Foundations for Lifelong Learning

Other Books by John Piper

Foundations for Lifelong Learning

Education in Serious Joy

John Piper

:: CROSSWAY®

WHEATON, ILLINOIS

Foundations for Lifelong Learning: Education in Serious Joy
© 2023 by Desiring God Foundation
Published by Crossway
   1300 Crescent Street
   Wheaton, Illinois 60187

Cover design: Jordan Singer

First printing 2023

Printed in the United States of America

Trade paperback ISBN: 978-1-4335-9370-3
ePub ISBN: 978-1-4335-9372-7
PDF ISBN: 978-1-4335-9371-0

Library of Congress Control Number:
2023941019

Crossway is a publishing ministry of Good News Publishers.

LB		32	31	30	29	28	27	26	25	24	23
15	14	13	12	11	10	9	8	7	6	5	4	3	2	1

To
Tim Tomlinson
Founding President
Bethlehem College and Seminary
2009–2021

Contents

Preface

THIS BOOK ATTEMPTS TO GIVE A GLIMPSE into the way we think about education at Bethlehem College and Seminary (www .bcsmn.edu). I hope students in high school, college, and seminary will read it.

But, as a matter of fact, the way we think about education makes the book relevant for all who want to grow in wisdom and wonder for the rest of their lives. Our aim is to equip students for lifelong learning. Therefore, this book is for anyone, at any age, who refuses to stagnate intellectually, spiritually, and emotionally.

Bethlehem College pursues this goal by focusing, as we say, on "the Great Books in light of the Greatest Book for the sake of the Great Commission." We agree with the late David Powlison when he explained why he loved the great novels and histories:

> Because you learn about people. You gain a feel for human experience. You come to understand riches and nuances that you could never understand just from knowing the circle of people you happen to know. You come to understand the

ways that people differ from each other, and the ways we are all alike—an exceedingly valuable component of wisdom. You become a bigger person with a wider scope of perception. All those things you come to know illustrate and amplify the relevance and wisdom of our God (see below, p. 36).

But what do we do with such books? And all books? And the Bible? And nature? And the world? That's what this book is about.

Six habits of mind and heart describe what we do with God's word and God's world—all of it. Observation. Understanding. Evaluation. Feeling. Application. Expression. Undergirded by a God-centered worldview, and guided by the authority of Scripture, we believe these six habits of mind and heart are the foundations of lifelong learning.

While Bethlehem College focuses on the great books in the light of the greatest Book, Bethlehem Seminary focuses with assiduous attentiveness on the great Book with the help of great pastor-scholars. We like to say that the seminary is "shepherds equipping men to treasure our sovereign God and sacred book for the joy of all peoples through Jesus Christ."

But whether for those in college, or in seminary, or in the marketplace, this book is about the foundations of lifelong learning beneath all those phases of life. The book is not about the subject matter of our curriculum, but what we *do* with it—indeed what we do with the subject matter of life. How do we deal with *all* subject matter in such a way that the outcome is ever-maturing disciples of Jesus who glorify him in every sphere of life?

Why we call it "Education in Serious Joy" is what the introduction is about. Such an education is a lifelong joy; it never ends. We are still on the road. We invite you to join us.

Introduction

Education in Serious Joy

THIS BOOK IS FOR SERIOUS seventy-somethings and seventeen-year-olds, and everybody in between, who share our excitement about what we call "education in serious joy." It is the overflow of our exuberance with the habits of mind and heart that we are trying to build into our lives and the lives of those we teach. We believe these habits are the pursuit of a lifetime, and therefore relevant for every stage of life.

Serious Joy

In our way of thinking, "serious joy" is not an oxymoron. "Serious joy" is not like "hot winters" or "cold summers." It's what the apostle Paul was referring to when he used the phrase "sorrowful, yet always rejoicing" in 2 Corinthians 6:10. We believe this is really possible. It's the experience of people whose love is big enough to weep with those who weep and rejoice with those who rejoice—even at the same time, if not in the same way.

These are the kind of people we want our students—we want you, young and old—to be. Most readers probably have enough people in their life that someone is always happy and someone is always sad. So every shared happiness happens while there is sadness. And every shared sadness happens while there is happiness. When you rejoice while someone is weeping (for there is no other time in this world), this will be "serious joy." Not sullen joy. Not morose joy. Not gloomy joy. But *serious* joy. Being serious is not the opposite of being glad. It's the opposite of being oblivious, insensible, superficial, glib.

Joy So Prominent?

Why do we make joy so prominent in our understanding of education? Why do we even have the phrase "education in serious *joy*"? The reason has to do with the ultimate questions of why the world exists and why we exist in it. We believe that everything in this universe was created by Jesus Christ. He owns it. He holds it in existence. It exists to put his greatness and beauty and worth (his glory) on display for the everlasting enjoyment of his people.

In fact, we believe that our joy in treasuring Christ *above* all things, and *in* all things, is essential in displaying his glory. Education is the process of growing in our ability to join God in this ultimate purpose to glorify Jesus Christ. That's why we give joy such a prominent place in our understanding of education. That's why we have a phrase like "education in serious joy."

Biblical Pillar

The biblical pillar for this understanding of our existence is Colossians 1:15–17:

[Christ] is the image of the invisible God, the firstborn of all creation. For *by him* all things were created, in heaven and on earth, visible and invisible, whether thrones or dominions or rulers or authorities—all things were created through him and *for him*. And he is before all things, and *in him* all things hold together.

Christ is the beginning, the middle, and the end. He is Creator, sustainer, and goal. The words "created *for* him" do not mean for his improvement. He doesn't have deficiencies that need remedying by creation. "*For* him" means for the praise of his glory (cf. Eph. 1:6). His perfection and fullness overflowed in creation to communicate his glory to the world.

He made it all. So he owns it all. "The earth is the Lord's, and the fullness thereof" (1 Cor. 10:26). Abraham Kuyper, who founded the Free University of Amsterdam in 1880, said in one of his most famous sentences, "There is not a square inch in the whole domain of our human existence over which Christ, who is Sovereign over all, does not cry, 'Mine!'"[1] As with all ownership, therefore, the world exists for the purposes of the owner. That is, for the glory of Christ.

That is the deepest foundation of education in serious joy: all things *were made* by Christ, *belong to* Christ, and *exist for* Christ. Humans exist to magnify Christ's worth in the world. But he is not magnified as he ought to be where humans are not satisfied in him as they ought to be—satisfied in him *above* all things, and *in* all things. Therefore joy, serious joy, is at the heart of Christ-exalting education.

---

1 Abraham Kuyper, *Abraham Kuyper: A Centennial Reader*, ed. James D. Bratt (Grand Rapids, MI: Eerdmans, 1998), 488.

Soul Satisfied, Christ Magnified

If that's a new thought for you—namely, Christ being magnified by our being satisfied in him—be assured its roots go back to the Bible. Paul said that his eager expectation and hope was that Christ would be magnified by his death (Phil. 1:20). Then he explained how this would happen: "for to me . . . to die is gain" (1:21). In what sense would his death be gain? He answers: "My desire is to depart and be with Christ, for that is far better" (1:23). Death is gain because death is "better"—that is, death brings a more immediately satisfying closeness to Christ.

How then will Paul magnify Christ by his death? By experiencing Christ as gain—as satisfying—in his death. Christ will be magnified by Paul's being more satisfied in Christ than in the ordinary blessings of life. This is why we think serious joy is essential to Christ-magnifying education. Christ is *magnified* in us by our being *satisfied* in him, especially in those moments when the satisfactions of this world are taken away.

We are not the first to draw out this essential truth from Scripture. It was pivotal, for example, in the thinking of Jonathan Edwards, the brilliant eighteenth-century pastor and theologian in New England. Here is how Edwards said it:

> God glorifies Himself toward the creatures also in two ways: 1. By appearing to . . . their understanding. 2. In communicating Himself to their hearts, and in their rejoicing and delighting in, and enjoying, the manifestations which He makes of Himself. . . . *God is glorified not only by His glory's being seen, but by its being rejoiced in.* When those that see it delight in it, God is

more glorified than if they only see it. His glory is then received by the whole soul, both by the understanding and by the heart. . . . He that testifies [to] his idea of God's glory [doesn't] glorify God so much as he that testifies also [to] his approbation of it and his delight in it.[2]

There it is: "God is glorified . . . by [his glory] being rejoiced in." The difference between Edwards's expression and the way we like to say it is that ours rhymes: "God is most *glorified* in us when we are most *satisfied* in him." Christ's worth is magnified when we treasure him *above* all things and *in* all things.

Joy in a World of Suffering

This happens in the real world of suffering—*our* suffering and the suffering of *others*. Christ's worth shines the more brightly when *our* joy in him endures through pain. But what about the suffering of *others*? How does their suffering relate to our joy in Christ? We start with this observation: Christ-exalting joy in us is a living, restless, expanding reality. Then we observe this remarkable fact about our joy: it becomes greater in us when it expands to include others in it. So when we see the suffering of others, the effect it has on us is to draw out our joy in the form of compassion that wants others to share it. Joy in Christ is like a high-pressure zone in a weather system. When it gets near a low-pressure zone of suffering, a wind is created that blows from the high-pressure zone to the low-pressure zone trying to fill it with relief and joy. This wind is called love.

2   Jonathan Edwards, *The "Miscellanies,"* vol. 13, *The Works of Jonathan Edwards* (New Haven, CT: Yale University Press, 1994), 495, miscellany 448; emphasis added.

This is what happened among the Christians in Macedonia: "In a severe test of affliction, their abundance of joy . . . overflowed in a wealth of generosity" (2 Cor. 8:2). First, joy in the gospel. Next, affliction that does not destroy the joy. Then, the overflow of that joy to others in generosity. That overflow is called love. Paul assumes that without the expanding impulse of joy toward others in need, there would be no love.

Putting it all together, I would say that the great purpose of lifelong learning—education in serious joy—is to magnify Christ by enjoying him *above* all things and *in* all things, with the kind of overflowing, Christlike joy, that is willing to suffer as it expands to include others in it. I know that's a complex sentence. Please read it again slowly and let it sink in. The name for that process—the aim of lifelong learning—is love (cf. 2 Cor. 8:8).

Enjoying Christ *in* All Things

At least four times in the preceding paragraphs I have said that we should enjoy Christ not only *above* all things, but also *in* all things. Why do I say it like that? The first (enjoying Christ *above* all things) is obvious: if we prefer anything above Christ, we are idolaters. If he is not our supreme treasure, we devalue him. Jesus said, "Whoever loves father or mother more than me is not worthy of me, and whoever loves son or daughter more than me is not worthy of me" (Matt. 10:37). Paul said, "I count everything as loss because of the surpassing worth of knowing Christ Jesus my Lord" (Phil. 3:8).

But why do we say that the aim of lifelong learning is to enjoy Christ *in* all things? One reason is that God created the material world so that we would see him and savor him *in* it—the world itself for what it is. God did not create the pleasures of the world as temptations to idolatry. They have become that, because of sin. After the fall of the world into sin, virtually every good can be misused to replace Christ as our greatest treasure.

Sex and Food as Revelation

This is not how it was from the beginning. And this is not how it should be for those who are being made new in Christ. We know this because of the way the apostle Paul speaks about the enjoyment of created things—like food in moderation, and sex in marriage. In 1 Timothy 6:17, he says that God "richly provides us with everything to enjoy." And he gets specific with regard to food and sex in 1 Timothy 4:3–5. He warns against false teachers who "forbid marriage and require abstinence from foods that God created to be received with thanksgiving by those who believe and know the truth. For everything created by God is good, and nothing is to be rejected if it is received with thanksgiving, for it is made holy by the word of God and prayer."

The enjoyments of sex in marriage and food in moderation are "richly provided" by God. They are not simply temptations. They are occasions for worship—namely, Godward thankfulness. They are "created . . . to be received *with thanksgiving*." Created things are "made holy by the word of God and prayer." "Those who believe and know the truth" receive them as undeserved gifts from God, feel gratitude to God for them, and offer God prayers of thanks that acknowledge him as the merciful giver. In this way, potential means of idolatry become holy means of worship.

This is what Paul has in mind when he says, "Whether you eat or drink . . . do all to the glory of God" (1 Cor. 10:31). Eating and drinking can *replace* God or *reveal* God.

Thus, education in serious joy aims for Christ to be magnified *above* and *in* all things. But not just "in all things" as the giver to be thanked; also "in all things" as the good to be tasted. God did not create the countless varieties of enjoyments of this world only to receive thanks. He also created those enjoyments to reveal something of himself in the very pleasures. "Oh, taste and see that the LORD is good" (Ps. 34:8) means that God gives his people a spiritual palate that can discern more of what God is like through the way he has revealed himself in the created world.

For example, honey reveals something of the sweetness of God's ordinances: they are "sweeter also than honey and drippings of the honeycomb" (Ps. 19:10). The rising sun reveals something of God's glorious joy: "The heavens declare the glory of God. . . . In them he has set a tent for the sun . . . which . . . runs its course with joy" (Ps. 19:1–5). The expectant thrill we feel at weddings is part of the pleasure we will have at the "marriage supper of the Lamb" (Rev. 18:7, 9; also Matt. 22:2). The morning dew reveals something of his tender coming to an unfaithful people: "I will be like the dew to Israel" (Hos. 14:5). The fruitful showers reveal something of God's life-giving mercies: "He will come to us as the showers, as the spring rains that water the earth" (Hos. 6:3). Light (John 8:12), thunder (Ps. 29:3), vultures (Matt. 24:28), lilies (Matt. 6:28), ravens (Luke 12:24)—these and thousands of other created things were made by God not only as gifts to elicit our thanks, but also as revelatory tastes of his perfections.

Focus of Our Study

When we speak of enjoying God *in* all things, the things we have in mind include both the *word* that God inspired and the *world* that God made. We have honey and sunshine and weddings and dew and rain and light and thunder and vultures and lilies and ravens. We know these things not first from God's *word* but from his *world*. Yet I cited a Scripture to go with each one. The significance of that interweaving of world and word is that it points to our answer to the question, What is the focus of our education in serious joy? What do we actually study? If God's aim in creating and governing the world is the display of his glory, where should we focus our attention? Where will we see the glory?

Our answer is that God has two books: his inspired *word* and his created *world*. This is what we study: the Bible, on the one hand, and the whole organic complex of nature and history and human culture, on the other hand. We are not the first to call creation and Scripture God's two books.

For example, in 1559, Guido DeBrès wrote the *Belgic Confession* for the Dutch Reformed churches and said in Article 2, under the title "The Means by Which We Know God":

> We know [God] by two means: first, by the creation, preservation, and government of the universe; which is before our eyes as *a most elegant book*, wherein all creatures, great and small, are as so many characters leading us to contemplate the invisible things of God, namely, his power and divinity, as the apostle Paul saith, Romans 1:20. All which things are sufficient to convince men, and leave them without excuse. Secondly, he

makes himself more clearly and fully known to us by his *holy and divine Word*, that is to say, as far as is necessary for us to know in this life, to his glory and our salvation.[3]

God created the world to communicate truth about himself. "His invisible attributes, namely, his eternal power and divine nature, have been clearly perceived, ever since the creation of the world, in the things that have been made" (Rom. 1:20). But man has suppressed the truth in unrighteousness (Rom. 1:18).

God's answer to this blindness was not to spurn the world, but to speak the word. He did this through the inspiration of Scripture and the sending of his Son. "Long ago, at many times and in many ways, God spoke to our fathers by the prophets, but in these last days he has spoken to us by his Son" (Heb. 1:1–2). We are rescued from our sin and blindness not by the revelation of God in the world, but by the heralding of the word of Christ: "Since, in the wisdom of God, the world did not know God through wisdom, it pleased God through the folly of what we preach to save those who believe" (1 Cor. 1:21).

God's Word Sends Us to God's World to Learn

But the decisive, saving power and authority of God's word does not cancel out God's world. The Bible gives the decisive meaning of all things. But the Bible itself sends us over and over again into the world for learning.

Consider the lilies; consider the birds (Matt. 6:26, 28). "Go to the ant, O sluggard; consider her ways, and be wise" (Prov.

---

3 Belgic Confession, Christ Reformed Church (website), accessed January 4, 2023, https://www.crcna.org/; emphasis added.

6:6). "The heavens declare the glory of God, and the sky above proclaims his handiwork" (Ps. 19:1). "Lift up your eyes on high and see: who created these?" (Isa. 40:26). And God says to Job, if you would be properly humbled before your God, open your eyes and consider the oceans, the dawn, the snow, the hail, the rain, the constellations, the clouds, and lions, and ravens, and mountain goats, and wild donkeys, and oxen, and the ostrich, and horse, and hawk, and eagle (Job 38–39).

In fact, think about the way the prophets and apostles and Jesus himself used language. They used analogies and figures and metaphors and similes and illustrations and parables. In all of these, they constantly assume that we have looked at the world and learned about vineyards, wine, weddings, lions, bears, horses, dogs, pigs, grasshoppers, constellations, businesses, wages, banks, fountains, springs, rivers, fig trees, olive trees, mulberry trees, thorns, wind, thunderstorms, bread, baking, armies, swords, shields, sheep, shepherds, cattle, camels, fire, green wood, dry wood, hay, stubble, jewels, gold, silver, law courts, judges, and advocates.

In other words, the Bible both commands and assumes that we will know the *world*, and not just the *word*. We will study the *general* book of God called *nature and history and culture*. And we will study the *special* book of God called *the Bible*. And the reason is that God has revealed his glory in both—and means for us to see him in both, and savor him in both, and show him to the world through both.

The two books of God are not on the same level. The Bible has supreme authority, because God gave the Bible as the key to unlock the meaning of all things. Without the truth of the Bible, the most brilliant scholars may learn amazing truths about nature. And we may read their books and learn from them. But without the special revelation of God, they miss the main point—that everything exists to glorify Christ. Not just some generic deity, but Jesus Christ, God's Son, the eternal second person of the Trinity. Without the special revelation of the gospel of Christ through Scripture, we remain blinded by sin. We do not see that we need a Savior and that Christ came into the world to save sinners. We do not see that the whole universe gets its ultimate meaning in relationship to him. When we miss the main reality, everything we think we have learned is skewed.

So, for Christians, lifelong learning—education in serious joy—is permeated by the study of the Bible. The Bible gives the key that unlocks the deepest meaning of everything else.

What Do We Do with God's Books?

If we are going to spend a lifetime focusing on the glory of God revealed in these two books—the word that God inspired and the world that God made—what should we do with these two books? We hope that you put out of your mind the thought that lifelong learning is about getting degrees behind your name (whether BA, MA, DMin, or PhD). They are incidental to real learning. We also hope that you don't think of education mainly as acquiring money-making skills. Of course, skills that enable you to function productively in your calling are important. But that is not mainly what *lifelong learning* is about. That is not mainly what we want you to do with God's world and God's word.

Our aim is to help you grow in the habits of mind and heart that will never leave you and will fit you for a lifetime of increasing wisdom and wonder through all the sweet and bitter providences of life. The well-educated person is not the one with degrees, but the one who has the habits of mind and heart to go on learning for a lifetime. Specifically, to go on learning what we need in order to live in a Christ-exalting way for the rest of our lives—whatever the vocation.

Six Habits of Mind and Heart

Lifelong learning for the glory of Christ calls for continual growth in six habits of mind and heart. These are the habits we seek to instill in our students so that their education does not stop when their schooling stops. These are the habits we seek to grow in ourselves. Helping you grow in these habits over a lifetime is why I have written this book.

These habits of mind and heart apply to everything we experience, but most importantly the Bible, because the Bible provides essential light on the meaning of all other reality. Growing in these habits can be summed up like this:

We seek to grow continually in the ability:

- to *observe* the world and the word accurately and thoroughly;
- to *understand* clearly what we have observed;
- to *evaluate* fairly what we have understood by discerning what is true and valuable;
- to *feel* with proper intensity the worth, or futility, of what we have evaluated;
- to *apply* wisely and helpfully in life what we understand and feel;

- to *express* in speech and writing and deeds what we have observed, understood, evaluated, felt, and applied in such a way that its accuracy, clarity, truth, worth, and helpfulness can be known and enjoyed and applied by others for the glory of Christ.

So the habits of mind and heart are:

- observation
- understanding
- evaluation
- feeling
- application
- expression

Whether you are looking at a passage in the Bible, or at the US Constitution, or the double helix of DNA, or a mysterious pattern of scratches on your car, the habits of mind and heart are the same.

1. Observation

We want to grow in our ability to *observe* the world and word accurately and thoroughly—as the world really is. We think it is crucial to see what is really there. If we fail in this, the failure is called delusion or blindness. Not to see what is really there with accuracy and thoroughness is to enter an illusory dreamworld. Such dullness to the facts before us is not a virtue. It is not only a fault in itself, but it also will result in the distortion of our understanding and evaluation.

2. Understanding

We want to grow in our ability to understand clearly what we have observed. Understanding involves the severe discipline of thinking. The mind wrestles to *understand* the traits and features of what it has observed. We may observe that certain kinds of violent crime dropped from one year to the next. Then comes the step of understanding: Why did this happen? Or we might observe in the Bible that four women are mentioned in Matthew's genealogy of Jesus—Tamar, Rahab, Ruth, and the wife of Uriah. Then comes the step of understanding. Why these four?

The aim of understanding when reading the Bible is to discern what the author is trying to communicate. We aim to think the author's thoughts after him. Or, more accurately, we aim to see the reality his thoughts are seeking to communicate. We aim to understand the author's purpose—ultimately, God's purpose. Otherwise, education simply becomes a reflection of our own ignorance.

3. Evaluation

We want to grow in our ability to evaluate fairly what we have observed and understood. We don't want to make value judgments prematurely. But neither do we want to shrink back from the judgments that must be made about truth and value on the basis of careful observation and accurate understanding.

Here is where our Christian worldview will make all the difference. We believe in truth and goodness and beauty. We believe that with the guidance of the Scriptures and the help of the Spirit, we can know the truth. Not infallibly but really. God's word is infallible. We are not. We believe that it is virtuous for right observation and right understanding to *precede* evaluation. The opposite is to say that our judgments do not need to be based on reality. This is called prejudice. We don't like it when people evaluate us without true observation and understanding. Therefore, we ought not do it to others.

4. Feeling

We want to grow in our capacity to feel properly in response to what we have observed and understood and evaluated. Our feeling should be in accord with the truth and worth of what we have observed and understood. If we have observed and understood a terrible reality like hell, our feeling should be some mixture of fear and horror and compassion. If we have observed and understood a wonderful reality like heaven, then our feelings should be joy and hope and longing.

I tried to show earlier in this introduction that God is glorified not just by being known, but also by being loved, treasured, enjoyed. Therefore, our emotional response to his glory (and what opposes it) has ultimate significance. Some people think that emotions are marginal in the task of education. We regard them as essential. This means that prayer and reliance on the heart-changing power of the Holy Spirit are indispensable for lifelong education in serious joy.

5. Application

We want to grow in our ability to apply wisely and helpfully what we have observed and understood and evaluated and felt. It takes wisdom, not just factual knowledge, to know how to wisely and helpfully apply what we are learning. Suppose a person is led by true observation and understanding and evaluation of his own life to feel earnestly that he should redeem the time (Eph. 5:16). Now what? What is the *application* of that insight? Only wisdom informed by Scripture and counsel and self-knowledge and circumstantial assessment and prayer-soaked meditation will lead to a fruitful application of Ephesians 5:16. A lifelong learner seeks to grow in the wise life-application of all he learns.

6. Expression

We want to grow in our ability to express in speech and writing and deeds what we have seen, understood, evaluated, felt, and applied. Yes, the line between application and expression is fuzzy. Expression, one could say, is a kind of application. But we hope to show why the habit of expressing what we know and feel through speaking and writing is worthy of a distinct focus. In a Christian worldview, the aim of expression is that our observation and understanding and evaluation and feeling and application will be made useful for others. In other words, as with other kinds of application, the aim is love. Throughout our lives, we long to grow in our effectiveness in expressing ourselves in a way that helps others see and savor and show the glory of God.

Invitation to Join Us

This brings us back to our original reason for being. God created his *world* and inspired his *word* to display his glory. A well-educated person sees the glory of God in the word that God inspired and in the world that God made. An educated person understands God's glory and evaluates it and feels it and applies it and expresses it for others to see and enjoy. That outward bent is called love. Therefore, the aim of lifelong learning is to grow in our ability to glorify God and love people. We think the six habits of mind and heart are a description of that process of growth. We invite you to join us.

1

Observation

We want to grow for a lifetime in our ability to observe the world and the word accurately and thoroughly.

BY *OBSERVING*, WE MEAN seeing or hearing or tasting or smelling or touching what is really there.

But that could be misleading. We don't mean that the only reality is what we experience by our five natural senses. The Bible speaks of the "eyes of the heart," not just the head. May "the *eyes of your hearts* [be] enlightened, that you may know what is the hope to which he has called you" (Eph. 1:18). There are unseen realities that Christians hope for.

This conviction pervades the Bible. Jesus indicted some people in his day because "seeing they do not see" (Matt. 13:13). Paul said that Christians in this age "walk by faith, not by sight" (2 Cor. 5:7). Hebrews 11:1 says that "faith is the conviction of things not seen." Peter says, "Though you have not seen [Christ], you love him" (1 Pet. 1:8). All these texts teach us that there is reality that is not immediately observable by our five senses.

But that does not mean it can't be known by "observation." We just need to make sure that we don't have a constricted view of observation that arbitrarily limits the kind of reality that we can observe. All five of our natural senses have spiritual counterparts. There is spiritual seeing, spiritual hearing, spiritual touching, spiritual smelling, and spiritual tasting.

Seeing

For example, Paul says in 2 Corinthians 4:4 that "the god of this world has blinded the minds of the unbelievers, to keep them from *seeing* the light of the gospel of the glory of Christ, who is the image of God." This implies that with *natural* sight, we see the facts of Christ's life as they appear in the story of the gospel. But Satan works in such a way that our *spiritual* sight fails to see in that story the "light . . . of the glory of Christ." God turns this around in 2 Corinthians 4:6: "God . . . has shone in our hearts to give the light of the knowledge of the glory of God in the face of Jesus Christ." In other words, natural seeing has its counterpart in spiritual seeing.

Hearing

Paul says that "faith comes from hearing, and hearing through the word of Christ" (Rom. 10:17). But why is it that many hear and do *not* have faith? Because, Jesus said, "hearing they do not hear" (Matt. 13:13). They hear the words, but they do not hear the voice of Christ. They do not discern the authenticating voice of the shepherd. "The sheep follow him, for they know his voice" (John

10:4). When Jesus said, "If anyone has ears to hear, let him hear" (Mark 4:23), he meant that natural ears have their counterpart in spiritual ears. There is natural hearing and spiritual hearing.

Touching

The apostle John spoke of touching Jesus Christ who is the embodiment of eternal life: "That which was from the beginning, . . . which we have . . . touched with our hands, . . . the eternal life, which was with the Father and was made manifest to us" (1 John 1:1–2). It is as though there were spiritual eyes in the fingers of the apostles—as if touching was seeing.

Jesus spoke just that way when he said to the frightened apostles after the resurrection, "Touch me, and *see*. For a spirit does not have flesh and bones as you see that I have" (Luke 24:39). And again he said to doubting Thomas, "Put your finger here, and *see* my hands. . . . Do not disbelieve, but believe" (John 20:27). Touch and *see*. There is a natural touching that does not "observe" who Christ is, and there is a spiritual touching that falls down and says, "My Lord and my God!" (John 20:28).

Smelling

There is a spiritual smelling that discerns the fragrance of Christ. Paul said, "Through us [God] spreads the *fragrance* of the knowledge of [Christ] everywhere. For we are the *aroma* of Christ to God among those who are being saved and among those who are perishing, to one a fragrance from death to death, to the other a fragrance from life to life" (2 Cor. 2:14–16). The point is that there is true spiritual discernment (smell) of Christ as life-giving, and there is the failure of that discernment which only "smells" Christ as death.

Tasting

When we think of spiritual tasting, we might be tempted to think of the Lord's Supper and the tasting of the actual material bread and cup. That would not be wrong. But the New Testament does not make that connection. Rather Peter says, to born-again Christians, "Like newborn infants, long for the pure spiritual milk, that by it you may grow up into salvation— if indeed you have *tasted* that the Lord is good" (1 Pet. 2:2–3). When we are born again, it's as though our hearts are given new tastebuds that can taste the sweetness of Christ and his love for us. As with touching, it's as though there are eyes in the tastebuds of the soul: "Oh, taste and *see* that the LORD is good!" (Ps. 34:8).

No Merely Natural World

When we define *observing* as seeing, hearing, tasting, smelling, and touching what is really there, we don't confine this act of observing to natural, physical acts of the senses. In fact, we believe that all of the material world, because it is created by a self-revealing God, reveals something of God not only to our natural senses but also to our spiritual senses—if they are alive. As Jonathan Edwards wrote:

> God is infinitely the greatest being . . . ; all the beauty to be found throughout the whole creation is but the reflection of the diffused beams of that being who hath an infinite fullness of brightness and glory.[1]

---

1   Jonathan Edwards, *Two Dissertations: The Nature of True Virtue*, ed. Paul Ramsey, vol. 8, *The Works of Jonathan Edwards* (New Haven, CT: Yale University Press, 1989), 550–51.

The natural beauty of creation reveals the spiritual beauty of God. Poets have tried to capture the reality of those "diffused beams" of God's reality in what he has made. For example, Gerard Manley Hopkins wrote in his famous poem "God's Grandeur":

> The world is charged with the grandeur of God.
>   It will flame out, like shining from shook foil.[2]

Elizabeth Barrett Browning pointed to the same divine penetration of material creation in her epic poem *Aurora Leigh*, written in 1856:

> Natural things
> And spiritual,—who separates those two
> In art, in morals, or the social drift
> Tears up the bond of nature and brings death,
> Paints futile pictures, writes unreal verse,
> Leads vulgar days, deals ignorantly with men,
> Is wrong, in short, at all points. . . .
> No pebble at your foot, but proves a sphere;
> No chaffinch, but implies the cherubim;
> And (glancing on my own thin, veinèd wrist),
> In such a little tremor of the blood
> The whole strong clamour of a vehement soul
> Doth utter itself distinct. Earth's crammed with heaven,
> And every common bush afire with God;

2 Gerard Manley Hopkins, "God's Grandeur" Poetry Out Loud, accessed June 20, 2023, https://www.poetryoutloud.org/.

But only he who sees, takes off his shoes,
The rest sit round it and pluck blackberries.[3]

There is no merely natural world. Everything in the world shines with the luster of divinity, and echoes the voice of eternity, and is scented with the fragrance of heaven, and seasoned with the spice of God's wisdom, and bears the texture of his character.

If we are fully alive to God's world, every act of seeing, hearing, smelling, tasting, and touching will be both natural and supernatural. We will see the thing God made, and the God-like reality it reveals. Everything that God created unveils something of God, if we only have the natural and spiritual powers of observation to detect it. This is why God gave us five natural senses, and why all of them have spiritual counterparts that come alive when we are born again. Then it can be said that seeing we see, and hearing we hear.

Eternal Significance of the Material World

It would be a serious mistake, however, to conclude from what we have said so far that the importance of the natural world disappears when supernatural glimpses of God appear. The created things of this world are not like annoying curtains that need to be thrown aside to see the concealed glory. If you throw aside the sun, the radiance of God in it vanishes (Ps. 19:4–5). If you throw aside the thunder, the voice of God in it is silenced (Ps. 29:3).

3 Cited in "Earth's Crammed with Heaven," Stephen Crippen (website), June 24, 2018, https://www.stephencrippen.com/.

The created world is not incidental to God's self-revealing purposes, as if once we see him, we can dispense with the material world. God does not see it that way. He could have created a world without matter—without material things. He could have created only spirits with all the moral qualities that humans display. But he did not do it that way. In fact, given the exuberance of the vast diversity of created wonders, God surely delighted in creating material things—from human bodies to immeasurable galaxies. C. S. Lewis says:

> There is no good trying to be more spiritual than God. God never meant man to be a purely spiritual creature. That is why He uses material things like bread and wine to put the new life into us. We may think this rather crude and unspiritual. God does not: He invented eating. He likes matter. He invented it.[4]

Instead of preferring an immaterial spirit world, (1) God created matter. (2) He designed it to reveal (not conceal) something of himself. (3) He entered into matter as the God-man, Jesus Christ. (4) He communicated his word by means of matter (human language spoken and written). (5) He taught that, in some form, matter would exist forever. And (6) he commanded us to observe matter and learn what it teaches.

How We Know Matter Matters

Let's take those six affirmations of matter one at a time and let the Bible shed light on each one.

4   C. S. Lewis, *Mere Christianity* (San Francisco: HarperOne, 2001), 63–64.

1. God created matter.

> In the beginning, God created the heavens and the earth. (Gen. 1:1)

> God made the world and everything in it. (Acts 17:24)

> [He is the one] for whom and by whom all things exist. (Heb 2:10)

> [God] created heaven and what is in it, the earth and what is in it, and the sea and what is in it. (Rev. 10:6)

2. God designed every kind of matter to reveal (not conceal) something of himself.

> The heavens declare the glory of God. (Ps. 19:1)

> O LORD, how manifold are your works!
>> In wisdom have you made them all;
>> the earth is full of your creatures. (Ps. 104:24)

> He did not leave himself without witness, for he did good by giving you rains from heaven and fruitful seasons, satisfying your hearts with food and gladness. (Acts 14:17)

> What can be known about God is plain to [all humans], because God has shown it to them. For his invisible attributes, namely, his eternal power and divine nature, have been clearly

perceived, ever since the creation of the world, in the things that have been made. (Rom. 1:19–20)

3. God entered into matter as the God-man, Jesus Christ.

See my hands and my feet, that it is I myself. Touch me, and see. For a spirit does not have flesh and bones as you see that I have. (Luke 24:39)

In the beginning was the Word, and the Word was with God, and the Word was God. . . . And the Word became flesh and dwelt among us, and we have seen his glory, glory as of the only Son from the Father, full of grace and truth. (John 1:1, 14)

When the fullness of time had come, God sent forth his Son, born of woman. (Gal. 4:4)

In him all the fullness of God was pleased to dwell. (Col. 1:19)

In him the whole fullness of deity dwells bodily. (Col. 2:9)

4. God communicated his word by means of matter (human language spoken and written).

All Scripture is breathed out by God and profitable for teaching, for reproof, for correction, and for training in righteousness. (2 Tim. 3:16–17)

No prophecy of Scripture comes from someone's own interpretation. For no prophecy was ever produced by the will of
man, but men spoke from God as they were carried along by
the Holy Spirit. (2 Pet. 1:20–21)

I had much to write to you, but I would rather not write with
pen and ink. (3 John 13)

5. God taught that, in some form, matter would exist forever.
It is not temporary, as if it would be discarded when this age is
over. The following passages point to the material reality of Jesus's
resurrection body and the bodily resurrection of all Christians,
and the renewal, not the annihilation, of the material world.

[In his resurrection body] Jesus himself stood among them, and
said to them, "Peace to you!" But they were startled and frightened
and thought they saw a spirit. And he said to them, "Why are you
troubled, and why do doubts arise in your hearts? See my hands
and my feet, that it is I myself. Touch me, and see. For a spirit does
not have flesh and bones as you see that I have." (Luke 24:36–39)

For the creation was subjected to futility, not willingly, but
because of him who subjected it, in hope that the creation itself
will be set free from its bondage to corruption and obtain the
freedom of the glory of the children of God. (Rom. 8:20–21)

So is it with the resurrection of the dead. What is sown is per-
ishable; what is raised is imperishable. It is sown in dishonor;
it is raised in glory. It is sown in weakness; it is raised in power.

It is sown a natural body; it is raised a spiritual body [the same body, but much more]. (1 Cor. 15:42–44)

While we are still in this tent [earthly bodies], we groan, being burdened—not that we would be unclothed [bodiless spirits], but that we would be further clothed, so that what is mortal may be swallowed up by life [something not less than physical bodies, but more]. (2 Cor. 5:4)

[At his second coming, Christ] will transform our lowly [material] bodies to be like his glorious body, by the power that enables him even to subject all things to himself. (Phil. 3:21)

6. Therefore, God commanded us to pay attention to matter. It is not insignificant. It is not temporary. It is given eternal dignity since the very Son of God exists as the God-man forever. The two natures of Christ, divine and human, united in one person as Creator and created, is an eternal witness to God's intention that the created world be an everlasting witness to God's nature, like a diamond with innumerable facets providing us with endless discoveries of God's infinite fullness. The command to pay attention will be valid forever.

But *ask the beasts*, and they will teach you;
    the birds of the heavens, and they will tell you;
or the bushes of the earth, and *they will teach you*;
    and the fish of the sea will declare to you.
Who among all these does not know
    that the hand of the LORD has done this? (Job 12:7–9)

Go to the ant, O sluggard;
  consider her ways, and be wise. (Prov. 6:6)

Look at the birds of the air: they neither sow nor reap nor gather into barns, and yet your heavenly Father feeds them. Are you not of more value than they? . . . *Consider the lilies* of the field, how they grow: they neither toil nor spin, yet I tell you, even Solomon in all his glory was not arrayed like one of these. (Matt. 6:26–29)

In fact, as we saw in the introduction, we have a call to observe the world in the very way the prophets and apostles and Jesus himself use language. They use analogies and figures and metaphors and similes and illustrations and parables. In all of these, they constantly assume that we have looked at the world and learned about vineyards, wine, weddings, lions, bears, horses, dogs, pigs, grasshoppers, constellations—you get the idea. I don't need to finish the list (see p. 11).

Obvious: Something to Be Observed

Pause here and consider the obvious implication of what we have said—namely, that there is an objective world outside our subjective consciousness to be observed. God and his creation exist outside of me, independently of me. I don't—you don't—create God or his ways or his thoughts or his world. Those are simply givens. We either see them accurately or we deceive ourselves. Even if millions say the sun is not shining, it shines. And the tiny minority who sees it, and says so, is not foolish.

Why would we pause to say something so obvious? Because many today are ambivalent about believing in objective reality. On the one hand, when their own bank account is at stake, they insist on objectively real money and objectively real calculations. At that point, they insist that there is objective right and wrong. They will not tolerate a bank employee saying that a miscalculation doesn't exist just because he does not want it to exist. There is objective reality. Mathematical calculations are not a matter of preference.

On the other hand, many of those same people who say they believe in objective reality when their money is as stake deny that there is such objective reality in other areas of their lives, for example, whether there is such an objective, God-created reality as male and female, or whether one can make of one's sexual being whatever one likes. Carl Trueman describes the present situation like this: "We all live in a world in which it is increasingly easy to imagine that reality is something we can manipulate according to our own wills and desires, and not something that we necessarily need to conform ourselves to or passively accept."[5]

In 1947, C. S. Lewis described the same denial of objective reality. In his book *The Abolition of Man*, he cited some modern educators who claimed that observations about objective reality are really just expressions of subjective feelings. The educators said:

> When the man said, *This is sublime*, he appeared to be making a remark about the waterfall. . . . Actually . . . he was not making a remark about the waterfall, but a remark about his own feelings. What he was saying was really *I have feelings associated in my mind with the word "Sublime,"* or shortly, I have sublime feelings. . . . This confusion is continually present in language

5   Carl. R. Trueman, *The Rise and Triumph of the Modern Self: Cultural Amnesia, Expressive Individualism, and the Road to Sexual Revolution* (Wheaton, IL: Crossway, 2020), 41.

as we use it. We appear to be saying something very important about something: and actually we are only saying something about our own feelings.[6]

Over against this view, Lewis defends what he calls "the doctrine of objective value, the belief that certain attitudes are really true, and others really false, to the kind of thing the universe is and the kind of things we are." The kind of thing the universe is! Yes. There really is something there to be observed. We are not trapped in the tiny cell of our own egos with nothing but mirrors on the walls. The excitement of learning is really possible. There is a whole world of wonders to discover if we are humble enough to observe what is really there.

I hope that you can see why we devote so much emphasis to the foundational habit of lifelong learning called "observation." We really believe that there is something there to observe. It is not a creation of our own imagination. It is rooted in the absolute reality of God, and then in his creation of a real world—a world with such God-intended design that it actually communicates something of the reality of God himself.

We hope you also see how this is absolutely foundational to all the habits of mind that follow. If there is nothing objective to *observe*, there is nothing to *understand*, nothing to *evaluate*. And all our *feelings*, therefore, have no more validity than a blowing leaf. One person's admiration of sacrificial love and another's disgust are equally valid. Because there is no objective reality that would make one feeling more fitting than another.

6   C. S. Lewis, *The Abolition of Man* (New York: Macmillan, 1947), 13–14.

What Shall We Observe?

Even though I can't comment on every possible reality to observe, it may be helpful to mention a few, as a way of stirring up your desire to be as attentive as possible. Let's take our cues from the Bible itself.

Observing Yourself

Here we meet several paradoxes. One is that introspection is both necessary and dangerous. You need to do serious self-observation from time to time if you are to truly know yourself. Yet we all know that there is such a thing as "morbid introspection" because one can easily lose touch with the world outside oneself where real health and transformation is found.

Another paradox is that focusing on one's happiness or sadness, for example, as a way of truly observing the nature of happiness and sadness, does not work. C. S. Lewis explains:

> You cannot *study* Pleasure in the moment of the nuptial embrace, nor repentance while repenting, nor analyze the nature of humour while roaring with laughter. But when else can you really know these things? "If only my toothache would stop, I could write another chapter about Pain." But once it stops, what do I know about pain?[7]

Nevertheless, in spite of paradoxes and obstacles, we must do the best we can. Because the Bible calls us to self-observation:

7   C. S. Lewis, "Myth Became Fact," in *God in the Dock: Essays on Theology and Ethics*, (Grand Rapids, MI: Eerdmans, 1970), 65–66.

Let us test and examine our ways,
    and return to the LORD! (Lam. 3:40)

Thus says the LORD of hosts: Consider your ways. (Hag. 1:5)

Watch yourselves lest your hearts be weighed down with dissipation and drunkenness and cares of this life. (Luke 21:34)

Pay careful attention to yourselves and to all the flock, in which the Holy Spirit has made you overseers. (Acts 20:28)

Let a person examine himself, then, and so eat of the bread and drink of the cup. (1 Cor. 11:28)

Examine yourselves, to see whether you are in the faith. Test yourselves. Or do you not realize this about yourselves, that Jesus Christ is in you?—unless indeed you fail to meet the test! (2 Cor. 13:5)

Keep a close watch on yourself and on the teaching. (1 Tim. 4:16)

We have found that a well-balanced and honest observation of our own emotions, thoughts, motivations, and behaviors, while not losing sight of the forgiving mercies of God in Christ, is a vital key for understanding other people with true empathy and caution.

Observing Others

What an endless education there is in being a careful student of other people's behavior and how they express their emotions and thoughts. One of the marks of psychopathy is to be utterly out of touch with other people's emotions. And one of the marks of personal health and maturity is to be able to get inside someone's skin, so to speak, and to some extent grasp what they are thinking and feeling, all the while knowing how fallible we are. This is, in fact, a key to loving others as we ourselves would like to be loved.

When Hebrews 10:24 is translated, "Let us consider how to stir up one another to love and good works," it blunts the force of the original Greek, which says, literally, "Let us *consider each other* for the stirring up of love and good works." There's no *how* in the original; the direct object of "consider" is "each other." It is a call to study each other. Observe each other carefully enough that you can stir up each other's motivation to love.

Leaders come in for a special focus of observation. "Remember your leaders, those who spoke to you the word of God. Consider the outcome of their way of life, and imitate their faith" (Heb. 13:7). The apostle Paul knew the burden of being observed as a leader and did not shy away from it. "Be imitators of me" (1 Cor. 4:16; 11:1). "What you have learned and received and heard and seen in me—practice these things" (Phil. 4:9). And when people observe Paul and live after his pattern, he tells the rest to "fix your eyes on those who walk according to the example that you have in us" (Phil. 3:17).

Observing men and women in the varied affairs of life is one of the most interesting and fruitful aspects of lifelong learning. But it does have its limits. The book of Ecclesiastes documents the futility of merely observing human life under the sun:

"I applied my heart . . . to see the business that is done on earth. . . . I saw all the work of God, that man cannot find out the work that is done under the sun" (Eccl. 8:16–17; cf. 3:10–11).

Which reminds us that we need the help of others to observe human behavior with true insight. This happens for us largely through books, and through *the* book, the Bible. For example, Christian counselor and teacher David Powlison (1949–2019) explained how his own observation of human nature was profoundly deepened by reading great literature, especially novels and history. He mentioned Fyodor Dostoyevsky's *Crime and Punishment*, Alan Paton's *Cry, the Beloved Country*, and Mark Helprin's *A Soldier of the Great War*:

Of course, I love [them] in a different way than I love Scripture. But alongside Scripture, I most love novels and histories. Why? Because you learn about people. You gain a feel for human experience. You come to understand riches and nuances that you could never understand just from knowing the circle of people you happen to know. You come to understand the ways that people differ from each other, and the ways we are all alike—an exceedingly valuable component of wisdom. You become a bigger person with a wider scope of perception. All those things you come to know illustrate and amplify the relevance and wisdom of our God.[8]

---

8   David Powlison, "A Novel Every Christian Should Consider Reading," Justin Taylor blog, The Gospel Coalition, August 29, 2014, https://www.thegospelcoalition.org/. This quote from David Powlison is one of the reasons I love the pedagogical strategy of Bethlehem College with its motto: "Great Books in the light of the Greatest Book for the sake of the Great Commission" (https://bcsmn.edu/college/).

Nothing can replace Scripture as the infallible word of God about human nature. Therefore, lifelong learning will always be a combination of observing real people, reading the best stories and analyses of people, and going deep with God's witness to the deep things of human nature that we cannot know any other way. David Powlison was absolutely confident that the counsel of Christ was the decisive, indispensable, finally authoritative word of God over against the world. But he knew that the world was a treasure chest of discovery awaiting Christ as the key.

Observing the Word

The very existence of the Bible is a trumpet blast about the importance of learning to read. And learning to read means learning to observe letters that make up words, and words that make up phrases, and phrases that make up sentences, and sentences that make up paragraphs, and how all of that works to communicate reality. The most important argument for literacy all over the world is that God has revealed himself infallibly in a *book*.

The fact that the Bible is a book and the fact that it is inspired by God—those two facts are laden with implications for how to read the book. On the one hand, it is a book composed with ordinary human language that needs to be understood—it is, after all, a real human book. On the other hand, it is luminous with the supernatural light of divine glory. Which means that the Bible calls for more than your natural kind of reading. Not less. But more. Natural *and* supernatural. If either is missing, we will misread God's word.[9]

9 That's the main point of my book *Reading the Bible Supernaturally: Seeing and Savoring the Glory of God in Scripture* (Wheaton, IL: Crossway, 2017).

Jesus put a huge emphasis on reading the Bible correctly. Six times he said the astonishing and indicting words to the Jewish leaders of his day, "Have you not read?" (Matt. 12:3–5; cf. 19:4; 21:16, 42; 22:31). The implication was this: for all their reading and their knowledge of what they read, it is as though they had not read it. That is a serious warning and challenge to all of us: read God's word well. Don't play games with it. Don't read your own ideas into a text. Read God's ideas out of the text. Let Jesus's words be a summons to lifelong growth in reading well. And that means, first, observing well.

Reading Is Observing

One might think reading is a substitute for observing. You can observe a crime being committed, or you can read about a crime being committed. True. But reading is not a substitute for observing. It is the replacement of one kind of observing for another kind. If we observe the world only through books, even *the* book, we will not be authentic people. The Bible, and all great books, send us from books back to flesh-and-blood people. But if we never observe the world through books, especially *the* book, we will be very limited in what we can know.

The reason is that daily life, even if we are world travelers (which most people aren't), is so much more limited than the world that opens to us through books. Other worlds, other times, other ways of seeing, can be ours through what we read. And the Bible is the compass that keeps all our reading from unfruitful directions. Being saturated with the Bible enables us to test all things and hold fast the good (1 Thess. 5:21) in everything we read.[10]

10 Whole books have been written about the kind of observation that makes reading fruitful. We recommend Mortimer J. Adler and Charles Van Doren, *How to Read a*

Coming to Terms

In all careful reading, there are two basic acts of observation. The first is "coming to terms." If reading is to be fruitful, a reader must "come to terms" with an author. That means the reader and author must see the same meaning in the words that are used. To quote Mortimer Adler, "If the author uses a word in one meaning, and the reader reads it in another, words have passed between them, but they have not come to terms. . . . For the communication to be successfully completed, therefore, it is necessary for the two parties to use the same words *with the same meanings*—in short, to come to terms. When that happens, communication happens, the miracle of two minds with but a single thought."[11]

Relating Propositions to Each Other

Actually, that's not quite accurate. Accurate communication does not just depend on coming to terms. It depends as well, as Adler also says, on observing propositions and their relationship to each other. This is the second basic aspect of observational reading. Words or terms by themselves do not communicate anything clearly. We need a context. That context consists not only in other words, but in the grouping of words into sentences. When those sentences assert something, we call them propositions. It is absolutely crucial in reading to observe not only the words but also how they become propositions and how those propositions relate to each other. Until that happens, communication is only partial.

Book: The Classic Guide to Intelligent Reading (New York: Touchstone, 1972); Andrew Naselli, *How to Read a Book: Advice for Christian Readers* (Moscow, ID: Canon Press, 2024); Piper, *Reading the Bible Supernaturally* (see esp. chap. 23).

11 Adler and Van Doren, *How to Read a Book*, 96–97.

Most of us do this intuitively without thinking about it. That's good. But the treasures of the Bible, and the treasures of the best writing in general, will not reveal themselves without the mind's more consciously and carefully asking about what the propositions are and how they are related. For example, consider the propositions in Romans 1:14–17 (with the connecting words I've italicized):

> I am under obligation both to Greeks and to barbarians, both to the wise and to the foolish. *So* I am eager to preach the gospel to you also who are in Rome. *For* I am not ashamed of the gospel, *for* it is the power of God for salvation to everyone who believes, to the Jew first and also to the Greek. *For* in it the righteousness of God is revealed from faith for faith.

The "So" at the beginning of verse 15 means that Paul's eagerness to preach in Rome grows out of his sense of indebtedness to all people expressed in verse 14. But the "For" at the beginning of verse 16 shows that his eagerness to preach the gospel also stems from the fact that he is not ashamed of the gospel. And the "for" in the middle of verse 16 shows why Paul is not ashamed of the gospel: it is the power of God for salvation. And then the "For" at the beginning of verse 17 gives the reason that the gospel is the power of God, namely, that in it the righteousness of God is revealed. So, there are five propositions, and their relationships are signaled by the connecting words "so" and "for" (three times). This kind of observation in reading sets the stage for "understanding" in the next chapter.

When words become "terms," and when sentences become logically connected "propositions," then the miracle of understanding can happen—"the miracle of two minds with but a single thought."

Observing Jesus

In all our observing of the world and the word, the most important reality to see is Christ. This is why all creation exists. "All things were created through him and for him" (Col. 1:16). "For him" means that every created thing exists to put the excellencies of Christ on display. Not surprisingly, then, Jesus said that not only the world, but the whole Bible points to him as well: "Beginning with Moses and all the Prophets, [Jesus] interpreted to them in all the Scriptures the things concerning himself" (Luke 24:27).

Implicitly and explicitly the Bible tells us to *observe Jesus*. "Therefore, holy brothers, you who share in a heavenly calling, *consider* [observe carefully] *Jesus*, the apostle and high priest of our confession" (Heb. 3:1). Nothing is more important to observe in all our observing than Jesus himself, especially as he shines in "the light of the gospel of the glory of Christ" (2 Cor. 4:4).

How to Observe

Implicit in all we have said about the habit of observing are pointers for how to do it. But we will close this chapter simply by making some of them explicit.

1. Observe the word and the world humbly and prayerfully.

We are not God. We are not the measure of truth or goodness or beauty. God is. He has revealed himself profoundly in his world and decisively in his word. That reality is outside of us. We do not make it what it is. It is what it is. Ours is to see and wonder. Ours is not to create meaning, but to find it. All of this implies humility.

It also implies the need for God's help. We are finite, fallible, and fallen. Without God's merciful rescue through Christ, what we observe will be distorted by our own pride and fear and greed. Therefore, we pray. We ask that God would open our eyes to see what is really there. "Open my eyes, that I may behold wondrous things out of your law" (Ps. 119:18).

That same prayer is needed for all observation, not just biblical observation. For the sake of lifelong learning, let every day begin with, "O Lord, have mercy, for Christ's sake, and grant that I see truly today. Open my eyes at every point to see the reality that your word and your world are meant to reveal."

2. Observe the word and the world patiently and assiduously.

In the appendix to this book is a well-known story of Agassiz and the fish. For some of us, reading it was a pivotal moment in the discovery of the importance of patient, assiduous observation. It tells the story of Harvard professor Louis Agassiz (1807–1873) presenting an aspiring naturalist with a dead fish with the instructions to observe what he saw and report. After ten minutes, the student thought he had seen what there was to see. But when he reported to the professor, the response was, *keep looking*:

> "That is good, that is good!" he repeated, "but that is not all; go on." And so for three long days, he placed that fish before my eyes, forbidding me to look at anything else, or to use any artificial aid. "Look, look, look," was his repeated injunction.[12]

12 Horace E. Scudder, ed., *American Poems: Longfellow, Whittier, Bryant, Holmes, Lowell, Emerson; with Biographical Sketches and Notes*, 3rd ed. (Boston: Houghton, Osgood, 1879).

After three days, he had seen more than he ever dreamed. You might not think that a fish is worth three days out of your life. But I promise you, there are passages in God's word and glories in God's world that are worth three hours or three days of your closest observation. Most people make the mistake of thinking that if they can't see something worth seeing in a few minutes, then it's time to move on—or maybe it's time to open a commentary and let other people do the discovery for us. But many of us have learned that with patience and aggressive attentiveness, there is more to see than you ever dreamed.

The esteemed historian of American history David McCullough (1933–2022) knew the story of Agassiz and the fish, and kept the saying on his desk, "Look at your fish." McCullough told his students, "Insight comes, more often than not, from looking at what's been on the table all along, in front of everybody, rather than from discovering something new."[13]

Observation is active. Many of us have been misled into thinking that observing, looking, watching (like TV or online streaming) is passive. What there is to see will just happen to us. We tend to think that the thing watched is active, but we are passive.

That may be true for entertainment. But it is not true for lifelong learning. The human mind was not meant to be a sponge. It was meant to be energetically active in aggressively looking for the clues of meaning. The Christian mind hears the voice of conscience: *Look! Listen! Attend carefully to what you are seeing. Spot clues. Be aggressively observant. Be unremitting in your attentiveness. Be unwaveringly watchful. Make connections. Notice patterns. Ask questions.*

13 Cited in Austin Kleon, "Look at Your Fish," Austin Kleon (website), September 17, 2018, https://austinkleon.com/.

Yes, a Christian assumption lies behind this aggressive attentiveness. The assumption is that we are not on this planet to be passively entertained, but to be actively loving. We are actively looking at the world and the word; the aim is that we might live a wiser and more loving life. Observing the repetition of a phrase in a paragraph might point to a life-giving insight. The shape of the paw print in the snow might tell the hunter where his family's next meal is hiding. The tear in a woman's eyes might prepare you for a more fruitful counseling session. If we don't see what is really there, we won't serve as we ought.

3. Observe the word and the world accurately and thoroughly.

When Jesus said that "seeing they do not see, and hearing they do not hear" (Matt. 13:13), and when he asked the ever-reading religious leaders of his day, "Have you never read?" (Matt. 21:16), he was making clear that it is possible to see partially and inaccurately. From beginning to end, the Bible warns against being "deceived." "Do not be deceived" (1 Cor. 6:9; 15:33; Gal. 6:7; James 1:16). Which means, make sure that what you see is what is really there.

When we encourage you to observe *thoroughly*, we don't mean exhaustively. No one can do that except God. For finite people, we always have more to see. What we mean is: strive to see enough of what is there so that the conclusions you draw from it are not inaccurate. Thoroughness is seeing enough to confirm accuracy. The aim is not omniscience, but rather to draw out truth from observing what is really there in the word or in the world. Thoroughness means that we have seen enough so that there is good reason to think that what we have seen is really the way it is.

*4. Give special effort to observing what will help you
be fruitful in your various callings.*

There are innumerable realities to observe. No one but God can look at all of them, let alone look with aggressive attentiveness. We must be selective. We only have one life to live in this age. A third of it is spent sleeping. God urges us, "Look carefully then [observe!] how you walk, not as unwise but as wise, making the best use of the time, because the days are evil" (Eph. 5:15–16). "Walk in wisdom toward outsiders, making the best use of the time" (Col. 4:5).

Our callings determine our priorities for observation. Are you a parent? Do you have a parent? Are you a brother or sister? Mother? Father? Grandparent? Grandchild? Neighbor? Employee? Supervisor? Owner? Landlord? Scientist? Church member? Elder? Teacher? Coach? Citizen? Mayor? Each of your callings gives focus to what you spend your time observing—what parts of the *word* you observe most closely, what aspects of this *world* you study most carefully. Wherever God has placed you in your relationships is a calling on your life to work "not by the way of eye-service, as people-pleasers, but as bondservants of Christ, doing the will of God from the heart, rendering service with a good will as to the Lord and not to man" (Eph. 6:6–7).

When Paul says to Timothy, "Do your best to present yourself to God as one approved, a worker who has no need to be ashamed" (2 Tim. 2:15), the principle applies to all of us, not just to pastors and elders who teach God's word. The pursuit of excellence in our callings is not about impressing people. It's about honoring our Lord. We observe his word and his world to know the truth and to be wise in our service.

Blessed Eyes

The first and most basic habit of the heart and mind in our pilgrimage of lifelong learning is *observation*. It is a delight and a duty. The word and the world are given to us for our joy and for our fruitfulness.

Clyde Kilby (1902–1986), who did more than any other person to introduce C. S. Lewis to Americans, made resolutions for his own joy and healthy usefulness. One of them was to engage in a kind of observation that simply delights:

> I shall open my eyes and ears. Once every day I shall simply stare at a tree, a flower, a cloud, or a person. I shall not then be concerned at all to ask what they are but simply be glad that they are. I shall joyfully allow them the mystery of what Lewis calls their "divine, magical, terrifying, and ecstatic" existence.[14]

Such delight is a gift of God. In that moment of delight, we are not strategizing or planning. Self-conscious gladness is self-defeating. Nevertheless, the Christian heart knows that all God's gifts are enjoyed most fully when the gladness overflows for the good of others. This is why observation is also a duty. When we see God for who he is, really see him, the impulse to rejoice and the impulse to love are one. Then it may be truly said, "Blessed are the eyes that see what you see!" (Luke 10:23).

---

14 John Piper, "Clyde Kilby's Resolutions for Mental Health and for Staying Alive to God in Nature," Desiring God, August 27, 1990, https://www.desiringgod.org/.

2

Understanding

We want to grow for a lifetime in our ability to
understand clearly what we have observed.

BY SAYING "CLEARLY," we simply mean that we don't want to be muddleheaded. We are not satisfied with interesting observations from God's word or God's world if they leave us confused. We want to grow in our ability to see how things make sense—if they do. They might not. There are books and articles and emails that are not clear enough, or true enough, to make sense. There are things in God's world and in God's word that may be beyond our ability to make sense of them. We are not God. But the aim of lifelong learning is to grow in our ability to understand what we observe, and to understand as much as we can for the sake of living a life of joy that glorifies God and serves others.

What Do We Mean by Understanding?

As is often the case, illustrations are easier to give than definitions. We will get to illustrations in a moment. But it might be worth at least trying to provide a definition of *understanding*: Understanding is the mind's grasp of how things fit together to lead to a valid conclusion. I know this is vague. That's because it is trying to cover different situations—like behaviors while opening the mail, and changes in the weather, and propositions in the Bible. The common denominator in these three situations where understanding is needed is that there is a valid conclusion to be drawn and some things that fit together to get us there. Understanding is seeing how the things fit together to lead to that valid conclusion.

Now for the Illustrations

1. Suppose that you were opening the mail while standing beside your kitchen table. You opened a birthday card that was sent to you by some precious friends. Suppose they were observing you and saw you toss the card, without reading it, onto the kitchen table while you continue to open the mail. Would they understand the meaning of what they observed? They might think that the meaning was that the card has little significance for you, and you thought you didn't need to read it. It's no more important than the rest of the mail.

But that would be a complete misunderstanding. The true meaning is that this card means so much to you that you don't want to read it quickly while standing by the kitchen table shuffling through the mail. You want to save it and sit down with it in the living room and read it slowly and savor every line. That's the difference between observing and understanding. To understand, your friends would need to observe a while longer, including your lingering over the card in your living room chair. And it would help their understanding if they would take into account the evidence of a long and precious relationship.

In this illustration, the "valid conclusion" that matters is this: I love these friends and aim to read their birthday card in a focused and undisturbed and affectionate way. The "things that fit together to lead to that conclusion" are your behaviors, which at first are ambiguous—instead of reading it immediately while standing at the kitchen table, you toss it on the table and finish shuffling through the mail. Only later do you take the birthday card to the living room and read it slowly with great attention and affection. In this situation, *understanding* means grasping how your behaviors fit together to lead to the valid conclusion: you love your friends and value their card very highly.

2. The second illustration has to do with interpreting the weather and is taken from the teaching of Jesus.

> Jesus answered [the Pharisees and the Sadducees], "When it is evening, you say, 'It will be fair weather, for the sky is red.' And in the morning, 'It will be stormy today, for the sky is red and threatening.' You know how to interpret the appearance of the sky, but you cannot interpret the signs of the times." (Matt. 16:2–3)

When Jesus says, "You know how to interpret," he meant, "You can understand." And that understanding meant that the Jewish leaders grasped how the events in coloration of the sky leads to a valid conclusion. If the sky is red in the evening, the valid conclusion is fair weather. If the sky is red in the morning the valid conclusion is stormy weather. In other words, it is possible to speak of understanding events of nature (not just human acts), if we think of them as fitting together to point to a valid conclusion.

3. The third illustration of our definition of *understanding* is taken from the Sermon on the Mount. It focuses not on the way human behaviors or natural events fit together, but on the way written (or spoken) propositions fit together to lead to a valid conclusion.

> Ask, and it will be given to you; seek, and you will find; knock, and it will be opened to you. *For* everyone who asks receives, and the one who seeks finds, and to the one who knocks it will be opened. Or which one of you, if his son asks him for bread, will give him a stone? Or if he asks for a fish, will give him a serpent? If you *then*, who are evil, know how to give good gifts to your children, how much more will your Father who is in heaven give good things to those who ask him! *So* whatever you wish that others would do to you, do also to them, for this is the Law and the Prophets. (Matt. 7:7–12)

Understanding this teaching of Jesus means grasping how things (the propositions) fit together to lead to the valid conclusion. It is a double valid conclusion: We should ask (7:7)! And we should love (7:12)! Verse 7 is the command to ask. Verse 12 is the command to do unto others as you would have others do to you. I chose this illustration because most readers don't linger long enough to see the connection between verses 11 and 12—that is, between the certainty of God's giving good things, and Jesus's command to take the risk of radical love.

Between the imperative *ask, seek and knock* in verse 7 and the imperative of treating others the way you want to be treated in verse 12, four propositions lead to this double conclusion. First, "*For* everyone who asks receives" (7:8). Second, none of you fathers would give stones or serpents to your children when they ask for what they need (7:9–10). Third, you are evil (7:11a). Fourth, *therefore*, since God is not evil, it is virtually certain he will give what we need when we ask him (7:11b).

From these four assertions follows the double conclusion: you should ask your heavenly Father for what you need (7:7), and make the sacrifices necessary to love the way you want to be loved (7:12).[1]

In these three illustrations, we can see that *understanding is the mind's grasp of how things fit together to lead to a valid conclusion.* This definition applies to human behaviors and to natural events in God's world, and to propositions in God's word (or any other writings). Understanding is mainly perceiving relationships between things and how those relationships point to a valid conclusion.

Reality of Validity

You may recall that in chapter 1, concerning *observation*, we pointed out that we were assuming that there really was something there to observe. This may seem obvious, but, as we saw,

---

1 For those who would like to pursue the skill of finding and relating propositions to each other in Scripture the way I have done it here, I would recommend the online ministry called Biblearc.com. This is an amazing tool for Bible study that grew out of Bethlehem College and Seminary and the priority we put on rigorous attention to the text of Scripture. One of its tools, called "arcing," is explained and illustrated in the appendix of John Piper, *Reading the Bible Supernaturally: Seeing and Savoring the Glory of God in Scripture* (Wheaton, IL: Crossway, 2017), 395–411. See also Andrew Naselli, *How to Read a Book: Advice for Christian Readers* (Moscow, ID: Canon Press, 2024).

one of the destructive habits of the modern world is to deny that there is objective reality outside of us. Instead, the human self is capable of creating whatever reality suits our desires.[2] Now in this chapter, as we deal with understanding, we need to point out another obvious reality: there is such a thing as validity. There is such a thing as logic leading to valid conclusions.

We have assumed this in our definition of *understanding*: the mind's grasp of how things fit together to lead to a *valid* conclusion. What do we mean by *valid*, and why do we think such a reality exists?

A conclusion is valid if it flows logically from its premises. For example, here is a conclusion that is *not* valid: All dogs have four legs. This horse has four legs. *Therefore*, this horse is a dog. No, a horse is not a dog. That conclusion is invalid. Why? Because the conclusion does not follow from the premises. The premises are true. "All dogs have four legs," and "This horse has four legs." But the conclusion doesn't follow, because "All dogs have four legs" doesn't mean *only* dogs have four legs. So the fact that a horse has four legs doesn't mean it's a dog.

Sometimes this kind of reasoning (when it's valid) is called Aristotelian logic. The most famous Aristotelian syllogism reads, "All men are mortal; Plato is a man; therefore, Plato is mortal."[3] That is valid logic, or we could just say that it is logical, or reasonable, because the conclusion really does follow from the premises.

2   See chapter X footnotes 5 and 6. [Trueman and Lewis **will be added later]
3   In his *Prior Analytics*, Aristotle defines syllogism as "a discourse in which, certain things having been supposed, something different from the things supposed results of necessity because these things are so." The Internet Classics Archive (24b, 18–20), accessed May 26, 2023, http://classics.mit.edu/.

If it said, "All men are mortal; Plato is mortal; therefore Plato is a man," it would *not* be valid. For that conclusion to be valid, the first premise would have to be, "Only men are mortal." Then the syllogism would be valid. But the reasoning would be invalid because the first premise is false. It is not true that only men are mortal.

Some scholars say that Aristotelian logic is foreign to the Bible. They argue that the Bible reflects Hebraic thinking rather than Hellenistic (or Greek) thinking. They would say that the Bible does not have its roots in linear, Aristotelian (sometimes called "Western") logic.

I think those generalizations and distinctions are misleading and unhelpful. The problem is that Jesus himself assumed so-called Aristotelian logic, for example, in the text cited above about interpreting the weather. He says in Matthew 16:2, "When it is evening, you say, 'It will be fair weather, for the sky is red.' " What does that mean? It means that these Hebraic Pharisees and Sadducees are thinking in so-called Aristotelian syllogisms (without being aware of such terms).

Premise 1: Red skies in the evening portend fair weather.
Premise 2: This evening the skies are red.
Conclusion: Therefore, the weather will be fair.

That is a valid syllogism. Then, in the first part of verse 3, they show that they are thinking this way again. They say in the morning, "It will be stormy today, for the sky is red and threatening." Again, they are thinking in this so-called Western, linear way:

Premise 1: Red skies in the morning portend stormy weather.

Premise 2: This morning the skies are red.

Conclusion: Therefore, the weather will be stormy.

Jesus responded to this use of observation and reasoning, "You know how to interpret the appearance of the sky." In other words, you know how to use your eyes and your minds to draw valid, logical conclusions when it comes to the natural world. So, he *approves* of their use of such natural observation and logical deliberation.

Such logical reasoning is universally valid because it is rooted in the way God is. God is not the victim or slave of logic; he is the source and ground of it. Ultimately there is such a thing as validity because God is the ground of valid logic.

It grieves me when I hear people speak of cold and lifeless logic. In the Bible, logic is anything but cold and lifeless. Every "therefore" in the Bible (Greek *oun*, 498 times in the New Testament) is a doorway to life and love. That's what we just saw in the logic of Matthew 7:7–12. Being logical at Matthew 7:12 is entirely in the service of being loving. This logic is not cold. It is a furnace driving the engine of love. Jesus does not say "therefore" for nothing. God is a good Father and will give good things to his children who ask; *therefore*, love people! He means for us to see the logic, and think about it, and go back to the premises of God's fatherly care, and believe it, and be strengthened by it in the risky business of loving others. This is what logic is for. Such logic is not lifeless. It is lifegiving.

Beware of joining the chorus of unthinking voices who play off logic against love or imagination or experience, as though life can survive without logic. It can't. If logic disappears, the replacement will be raw power. Tyranny. And that has meant death for millions. For example, suppose you are charged with a crime. And suppose that at your trial you give three incontrovertible evidences that that you were not present at the time and place of the crime: You were teaching a class, and thirty students will testify to it. Your phone GPS record pinpoints your location, away from the scene, at the time of the crime. Two witnesses saw someone else of a totally different description commit the crime. You conclude that it is a clearly *valid* conclusion from these three evidences (premises!) that you are innocent and should go free. But when the time comes for the case to be decided, the judge says, "Your appeal to *logical validity*, sir, is an antiquated notion of cold and lifeless rationality. We do not believe in it. We find you guilty, and sentence you to death."

Both biblical reasoning in the mouth of Jesus and our own personal experience teach that the concept of validity, rooted in logic (which, in turn, is rooted in God), is not cold and lifeless. Rather, it fuels the furnace of love in God's word, and it provides the foundations of life and justice in society. Therefore, the effort to seek understanding by drawing out valid inferences from what we observe is not baseless. Just as the task of *observation* is rooted in objective reality which is really there to observe, so also the task of *understanding* is rooted in valid logic which really exists. Both objective reality and logical validity exist because they are rooted in God's character and creation.

What's at Stake in Right Understanding?

Before we turn to strategies for growth in the lifelong quest for understanding, let's have the Bible clarify what is at stake. Our experience is that if we immerse ourselves in what the Bible says about understanding, and then give our lives to pursuing such understanding, it turns out that we understand *everything* better. Honing our skills of understanding God's *word* fits us for understanding God's *world*—all of it. And it makes us serious because of what is at stake.

The Bible makes it clear that one can read (that is, observe the words on a page) and yet not understand. Jesus warned his contemporaries that Isaiah's prophecy was coming true before their eyes: "You will indeed hear but never understand" (Matt. 13:14). Therefore, Jesus cried out to the people, "Hear and understand" (Matt. 15:10). Not just hear. But hear *and* understand.

This is why the disciples said to Jesus, "Explain the parable to us" (Matt. 15:15). A huge difference exists between hearing (or reading, or observing) and understanding. It is unsettling to watch how many seemingly plain things Jesus said were not understood. For example, " 'The Son of Man is going to be delivered into the hands of men, and they will kill him. And when he is killed, after three days he will rise.' But they did not understand the saying" (Mark 9:31–32).

What is at stake in the failure to understand God's word in Scripture? What is at stake is the right knowledge of God and his word and his way of salvation. Right understanding is the only path to right knowing. Thus, the psalmist prays, "I am your servant; give me *understanding*, that I may *know* your testimonies!" (Ps. 119:125). Right understanding brings right knowledge. And without the right knowledge of God, we perish. "My people are destroyed for lack of knowledge" (Hos. 4:6). "My people go into exile for lack of knowledge" (Isa. 5:13). This is what is at stake: salvation or destruction.

Even where there is a zeal for God, it is not a saving zeal where knowledge fails. "Brothers, my heart's desire and prayer to God for [my Jewish kinsmen] is that they may be saved. For I bear them witness that they have a zeal for God, but *not according to knowledge*" (Rom. 10:1–2). They need to be saved because their zeal is not according to knowledge. It is possible to twist the words of Scripture, fail to understand, and be destroyed. "There are some things in [Paul's letters] that are hard to understand, which the ignorant and unstable twist to their own destruction" (2 Pet. 3:16).

But that is only half the picture of what is at stake in right understanding and right knowing. The other half is not the misery of missing the truth, but the joy of grasping it. "You make *known* to me the path of life; in your presence there is fullness of *joy*; at your right hand are *pleasures* forevermore" (Ps. 16:11). To know rightly is to rejoice forever. The right knowledge of God's promises is the ground of all our joy through suffering. "We *rejoice* in our sufferings, *knowing* that suffering produces endurance, and endurance produces character, and character produces hope, and hope does not put us to shame" (Rom. 5:3–5). So, what is at stake? If we *don't* have right understanding, there will be misery and destruction. If we *do* have right understanding, there will be gladness and everlasting joy.

How Then Shall We Seek Understanding?

No one is ever too old to grow in the ability to understand. We always have steps to take and efforts to make in the pursuit of grasping more of the pieces of God's world and how they fit together to point to his grand conclusion. Therefore, the brief suggestions that follow are for everyone, as God gives you strength.

1. Pray

I may as well say it now: *all* the habits of mind and heart should begin with deeply felt dependence on God expressed in prayer. "Apart from me you can do nothing" (John 15:5). This statement of Jesus is more far reaching than many think. Since he created and upholds the world (Col. 1:17; Heb. 1:3), it really means "nothing." As Acts 17:25 says, "God . . . gives to all mankind life and breath and everything." Everything! Through the universal creating and sustaining of Christ.

Therefore, right understanding is a gift of God. And he has told us often: "Ask, and it will be given to you" (Matt. 7:7). "If any of you lacks wisdom, let him ask God" (James 1:5). Five times the psalmist prays, "Give me understanding" (Ps. 119:169). "Give me understanding, that I may keep your law" (Ps. 119:34). "Give me understanding that I may learn your commandments" (Ps. 119:73). "Give me understanding, that I may know your testimonies!" (Ps. 119:125). "Give me understanding that I may live" (Ps. 119:144).

The apostle Paul models for us such prayers for understanding: "We have not ceased to pray for you, asking that you may be filled with the knowledge of his will in all spiritual wisdom and understanding" (Col. 1:9). "It is my prayer that your love may abound more and more, with knowledge and all discernment" (Phil. 1:9). "[I pray] that the eyes of your hearts [would be] enlightened, that you may know what is the hope to which he has called you" (Eph. 1:18). "[I pray that you] may have strength to comprehend with all the saints what is the breadth and length and height and depth, and to know the love of Christ that surpasses knowledge" (Eph. 3:18–19). Paul is profoundly aware that the riches of understanding God and his ways are a gift given in answer to the earnest prayers of God's people. James would rebuke many of us, "You do not have, because you do not ask" (James 4:2). Lifelong learning means lifelong praying.

2. Think

Recall that we defined *understanding* as the mind's grasp of how things fit together to lead to a valid conclusion. Thinking is what the mind does to attain that grasp. It is the mental effort to figure out how things fit together. J. Gresham Machen, one of the founding professors of Westminster Seminary, defined thinking like this:

> When any new fact enters the human mind, it must proceed to make itself at home; it must proceed to introduce itself to the previous denizens of the house. That process of introduction of new facts is called thinking. And, contrary to what seems to be quite generally supposed, thinking cannot be avoided by the Christian man.[4]

In other words, thinking is the effort to fit together facts that enter the mind by observation so that they make sense.

Someone might be thinking, *If understanding is a gift of God to be received through prayer, why are you suggesting that the human effort of thinking is so important?* The answer is that the Bible teaches us that God answers the prayer for understanding through the human means of thinking. Paul says to Timothy, "Think over

4 J. Gresham Machen, *What Is Faith?* (1937; repr., Edinburgh: Banner of Truth, 1991), 242.

what I say, for the Lord will give you understanding in everything" (2 Tim. 2:7). He does not say, "Since the Lord gives understanding, you don't need to think." And he does not say, "Since you gain understanding by thinking, you don't need to pray for God's gift." He says, in effect, pursue understanding by thinking, because that is the way God works to answer your prayer.

Proverbs 2:3–6 describes this paradox of human effort and divine gift even more energetically than Paul does:

> Yes, if you call out for insight
>   and raise your voice for understanding,
> if you seek it like silver
>   and search for it as for hidden treasures,
> then you will understand the fear of the Lord
>   and find the knowledge of God.
> For the Lord gives wisdom;
>   from his mouth come knowledge and understanding.

Call. Raise your voice. Seek. Search. And you will find. Because God gives. That's the paradox. His giving does not cancel out our striving. And our striving does not cancel out his giving. "*Think* over what I say, for the Lord will *give* you understanding in everything."

Paul underlines the crucial role of thinking in 1 Corinthians 14:20: "Brothers, do not be children in your thinking. Be infants in evil, but in your thinking be mature." Paul is keenly aware that there is childish, immature thinking, and there is mature thinking. "When I was a child . . . I thought like a child, I reasoned like a child. When I became a man, I gave up childish ways" (1 Cor. 13:11). This is why lifelong learning is so important. We never reach a point in this life when we can say, I have fully matured and need no more growth in my ability to think.

If there is room for growth in our love to God—which there always is—then there is room for growth in our thinking, because Jesus said we should love God with all our mind. "You shall love the Lord your God with all . . . your *mind*" (Luke 10:27). In other words, use all your mental powers of thinking to find truth and throw it as fuel into the furnace of your love for God. Make thinking serve loving.

All fruitful reading is thinking. Passive reading does not usually yield understanding. Active reading means thinking about what we read—that is, the intentional effort to fit the words and phrases and propositions and paragraphs together so that they lead us to a valid grasp of what the author is trying to communicate. That effort is called "thinking," and it consists mainly in asking questions of the text and trying to answer them by what we see. One of the most helpful books on this kind of active reading is Mortimer Adler's *How to Read a Book*. In it he says, "Reading a book on any level beyond the elementary is essentially an effort on your part to ask it questions (and to answer them to the best of your ability)."[5]

Rudyard Kipling (1865–1936) wrote this poem, supposedly, for his daughter in 1902. It illustrates the crucial role of asking questions in the task of active reading, that is, thinking:

> I keep six honest serving-men
> (They taught me all I knew);

5   Mortimer J. Adler and Charles Van Doren, *How to Read a Book: The Classic Guide to Intelligent Reading* (New York: Touchstone, 1972), 47.

Their names are What and Why and When
　　And How and Where and Who.
I send them over land and sea,
　　I send them east and west;
But after they have worked for me,
　　I give them all a rest.
I let them rest from nine till five,
　　For I am busy then,
As well as breakfast, lunch, and tea,
　　For they are hungry men.

But different folk have different views;
　　I know a person small—
She keeps ten million serving-men,
　　Who get no rest at all!
She sends 'em abroad on her own affairs,
　　From the second she opens her eyes—
One million Hows, two million Wheres,
　　And seven million Whys!

There are serious and humorous points to be made from this poem. A humorous one is that children can drive a parent crazy around four years old with never-ending questions that often defy answers, especially the *hows* and *whys*. But the more serious point is that Kipling amazes us by saying that six questions taught him all he knows! In other words, active reading and active interaction with the world mainly mean questions, questions, questions.

One point from this poem I would like to draw out is that too many Bible readers leave behind the childlike curiosity of *how* and *why.* I agree that *who* and *what* and *where* and *when* are valuable questions. But they are the questions that usually require the least thinking. And yet in Bible study, they are often as far as some people get. The really fruitful questions are *how* and *why. Why* does Jesus use a "therefore" to connect the Golden Rule in Matthew 7:12 with his Father's readiness to give us good things in answer to prayer (7:11)? *How* does God's fatherly care lead to self-denying love?

That kind of perplexity—the habit of asking questions—leads to hard thinking and wonderful discoveries. Adler presses this home: "Perhaps you are beginning to see how essential a part of reading it is to *be perplexed and know it.* Wonder is the beginning of wisdom in learning from books as well as from nature."[6] John Dewey (1859–1952) is reputed to have said something similar: "We never think until we are confronted with a problem." Asking questions is a way of posing problems to solve. Solving them is what we call "thinking."

One of the implications of this for lifelong learning is that we should regularly be reading books that are beyond what we already understand:

> *If you are reading in order to become a better reader, you cannot read just any book or article.* You will not improve as a reader if all you read only books that are well within your capacity. You must tackle books that are beyond you, or, as we have said, books that are over your head. Only books of this sort will make you stretch your mind. And unless you stretch, you will not learn.[7]

6 Adler and Van Doren, *How to Read a Book*, 123; emphasis original.
7 Adler and Van Doren, *How to Read a Book*, 339.

An exciting truth for the Christian is that the Bible is always over our head—in more ways than one. No matter how many years we have been reading it and studying it and thinking about it, we always have more to see and more to understand. If you form the habits of heart and mind described in this book, the Bible will be an inexhaustible well of wisdom and joy for a lifetime.

3. Embrace Unfamiliar, Biblical Categories of Thought

As we seriously attempt to put the parts of Scripture together so that they make sense and lead to a valid understanding of the author's intention, we run into conclusions that don't fit the way we usually think. We are not referring to things that break the rules of valid logic. We are referring to things that are so different from the way we have viewed the world, we don't see how they can be true.

That should not surprise us. In order for that not to happen, we would need to have a perfect way of viewing the world before we read the Bible. But one of the purposes of the Bible is to set right our wrong ways of viewing the world. As fallen sinners, we naturally see things in ways that are distorted and dishonoring to God (cf. Rom. 8:7–8; 1 Cor. 2:14). Therefore, as we observe accurately and thoroughly, and as we understand what we read honestly and clearly, we will need to let the text lead us to new and true valid conclusions, even when they seem foreign to us.

Here are a few examples of biblical truths that most fallen minds have no conceptual categories for before the Bible reshapes our way of seeing the world. I expect that some of these will be new to some of you, and hope that you will not reject them without serious consideration of what the Bible teaches.

That is what lifelong learning is for. I'll introduce the first seven and let the last three stand on their own. And if we run out of time here in this life, God will make things plain in the kingdom where all is light.

1. All persons are accountable for their choices, and all their choices are infallibly and decisively ordained by God.

> [He] works all things according to the counsel of his will. (Eph. 1:11)

> On the day of judgment people will give account for every careless word they speak. (Matt. 12:36)

2. It is not sin in God to will that there be sin.

> As for you, you meant evil against me, but God meant it [the evil acts of Joseph's brothers] for good. (Gen. 50:20)

3. What God decrees will come to pass is not always the same as what he commands that we do, and may indeed be the opposite.

> For example, he may command, "You shall not murder" (Ex. 20:13), and decree that his Son be murdered: "It was the will of the LORD to crush him" (Isa. 53:10).

4. God's ultimate goal is the exaltation and display of his own glory, and this is at the heart of what it means for him to love us.

Now, Father, glorify me in your own presence with the glory
that I had with you before the world existed. (John 17:5)

Father, I desire that they also, whom you have given me, may
be with me where I am, to see my glory. (John 17:24)

5. Sin is not to be defined primarily as what hurts man but
what belittles God by expressing unbelief or indifference to his
superior worth.

My people have committed two evils:
they have forsaken me,
   the fountain of living waters,
and hewed out cisterns for themselves,
   broken cisterns that can hold no water." (Jer. 2:13)

6. God is perfectly just and orders the complete destruction of
the inhabitants of Canaan.

Shall not the Judge of all the earth do what is just?
(Gen. 18:25)

But in the cities of these peoples that the LORD your
God is giving you for an inheritance, you shall save
alive nothing that breathes. (Deut. 20:16)

7. Key to the Christian life is learning the secret of acting in such
a way that our acts are done as the acts of another.

Walk by the Spirit. (Gal. 5:25)

By the Spirit . . . put to death the deeds of the body. (Rom. 8:13)

8. Christians have died but go on living.

I have been crucified with Christ. . . . The life I now live in the flesh I live by faith in the Son of God. (Gal. 2:20)

9. Jesus was conceived in his mother without an earthly father.

The virgin shall conceive and bear a son. (Matt. 1:23)

10. Jesus, the Son of God, never had a beginning.

Jesus said, "Before Abraham was, I am." (John 8:58)

All ten of these statements run counter to the ordinary way most people think. Which means that in our effort to understand God's word, we humbly should be willing to embrace unfamiliar, biblical categories of thought.

4. Obey through Hardship What You Understand

God has made humans in such a way that the *mind* sees more clearly when the *will* inclines to truth. We learn this from what Jesus says in John 7:17: "If anyone's will is to do God's will, he will know whether the teaching is from God or whether I am speaking on my own authority." Notice the connection between willing and knowing. If anyone wills, he will know. It should not surprise us that the mind more readily understands what is true when the will is not resisting it. Therefore, obedience to the truth we already know is a biblical path to knowing more.

If you want to understand more than old people, obey:

> I understand more than the aged,
>   for I keep your precepts. (Ps. 119:100)

If you want to have a good understanding, obey:

> The fear of the LORD is the beginning of wisdom;
>   all those who practice it have a good
>   understanding.
> His praise endures forever! (Ps. 111:10)

If you want wisdom and understanding, obey:

> Behold, the fear of the Lord, that is wisdom,
>   and to turn away from evil is understanding. (Job 28:28)

If you want to be wise and understanding, obey:

> Who is wise and understanding among you? By his good conduct let him show his works in the meekness of wisdom. (James 3:13)

The reason I titled this section "Obey through *Hardship* What You Understand" is that God has designed us not only to see *more* truth when we obey what we *already* see, but also to see more when that obedience endures affliction. "It is good for me that I was afflicted, that I might learn your statutes" (Ps. 119:71). Affliction is a key to understanding God's statutes.

Everyone who has been a Christian for some time knows this: times of prosperity and health and ease are a precious gift of God designed to enlarge our thankfulness, but times of pain and sorrow are designed to reveal things about the sustaining grace and goodness and preciousness of God we could taste no other way.

Martin Luther (1483–1546) speaks perhaps more forcefully than anyone about the necessity of affliction in becoming a good interpreter of the Bible:

> I want you to know how to study theology in the right way. I have practiced this method myself. . . . Here you will find three rules. They are frequently proposed throughout Psalm [119] and run thus: *Oratio, meditatio, tentatio* (prayer, meditation, trial).[8]

And *trials* he called the touchstone. Trials, he writes, "teach you not only to know and understand but also to experience how right, how true, how sweet, how lovely, how mighty, how comforting God's Word is: it is wisdom supreme."[9] He proved the value of trials over and over again in his own experience:

> As soon as God's Word becomes known through you, the devil will afflict you, will make a real doctor of you, and will teach

8   Ewald M. Plass, ed., *What Luther Says: An Anthology*, vol. 3 (St. Louis, MO: Concordia, 1959), 1359.
9   Plass, *What Luther Says*, 1360.

you by his temptations to seek and to love God's Word. For I myself . . . owe my papists many thanks for so beating, pressing, and frightening me through the devil's raging that they have turned me into a fairly good theologian, driving me to a goal I should never have reached.[10]

This may be the most crucial strategy of all in our lifelong quest to grow in our ability to understand what we observe. How many people in the world know the secret that repentance is a key to reading? Or to put it positively: obedience, especially through hardship, will open windows of understanding that make us the kind of people God uses for the good of the world, the glory of his name, and the joy of our souls.

5. Belong to a Bible-Saturated Church

The point of drawing attention to the importance of being embedded in a Bible-saturated church is that God intends for our lifelong growth in understanding to be a community project. The Bible does not encourage solitary Christians in their quest for understanding.

Philip, one of the first officers in the early church (Acts 6:5), was sent by the Holy Spirit to meet a chariot carrying an Ethiopian eunuch who served his queen Candace. He was leaving Jerusalem and was reading the prophet Isaiah as he traveled. Philip heard him and approached and asked, " 'Do you understand what you are reading?' He answered, 'How can I, unless someone guides me?' . . . Then Philip opened his mouth, and

10 Plass, *What Luther Says*, 1360.

beginning with this Scripture, he told him the good news about Jesus" (Acts 8:26–35).

The eunuch needed help to understand. This is not an indictment of the eunuch. His need for help was not a sin. It may be humbling to us, but it is God's plan that we be partly dependent on the help of others in our quest for understanding. I say "partly" because it is also clear that God expects us to read and think for ourselves. But it is not for nothing that Christ has given to his church

> shepherds and teachers, to equip the saints for the work of ministry, for building up the body of Christ, until we all attain to the unity of the faith and of the knowledge of the Son of God, to mature manhood, to the measure of the stature of the fullness of Christ. (Eph. 4:11–13)

Christ is the chief "Shepherd and Overseer" of his earthly flock (1 Pet. 2:25). But he has appointed undershepherds, pastors, and teachers to feed the sheep by helping them understand the word of God. Then, when they have done this, the "chief Shepherd appears" and awards "the unfading crown of glory" (1 Pet. 5:4). We all are needy sheep, even pastors and teachers. And none of us should resent having to learn from another sheep.

God has arranged the church so that there is mutual dependence. "The eye cannot say to the hand, 'I have no need of you,' nor again the head to the feet, 'I have no need of you'" (1 Cor. 12:21). All of us are designed to be dependent on other believers in various ways. It humbles us and calls attention to the wisdom of Christ in the way he builds his church.

The leaders of the church are to follow in the steps of the Levites in Ezra's day:

> The Levites helped the people to understand the Law, while the people remained in their places. They read from the book, from the Law of God, clearly, and they gave the sense, so that the people understood the reading. (Neh. 8:7–8)

None of us ever outgrows our need for help. If you are reading this book, you evidently are happy to affirm that. We who teach these habits of mind and heart know that we are standing on the shoulders of faithful teachers and scholars. Many of them are long dead, and though dead, they keep on speaking because God has been merciful to preserve great books to help us. We are thankful.

Lifelong Privilege of Understanding More

Yes, we have put a great emphasis on observing and understanding by using your own God-given powers of seeing and thinking. These habits of mind and heart are, of course, even necessary in reading books that help us understand the Bible. There is no escaping the joy and challenge of observing and understanding that God has assigned to us: "Think over what I say, and the Lord will give you understanding in everything" (2 Tim. 2:7). It is a lifelong privilege. I hope you will join me in it.

3

Evaluation

*We want to grow for a lifetime in our
ability to evaluate fairly and correctly what
we have observed and understood.*

BY *EVALUATE*, I MEAN MAKE judgments about the truth or
goodness or beauty or worth of what we have observed and
understood. The attempt to go through life without passing
judgments of true or false, good or bad, right or wrong, beautiful
or ugly, valuable or worthless (and the gradations in between) is
impossible. Not only that, but there are three positive reasons for
evaluating things fairly and correctly. It honors God, shows love
to people, and deepens our own joy. If that is true (and I will
try to show that it is), then we need to think carefully about
why that is the case, and how to go about evaluating in a way
that acknowledges its necessity, and is not irreverent, unloving,
or unsatisfying.

Impossible to Not Evaluate

The reason it is impossible to go through life without evaluating—without making judgments—is that our will is almost never neutral. When confronted with a claim of truth, or a choice of action, or an object to possess, or artwork to look at, the will almost always inclines one way or the other without needing any conscious push. It affirms or denies, approves or disapproves, is pleased or displeased, likes or dislikes, is attracted or repelled, prefers or does not prefer, desires or does not desire. True neutrality, with no leaning at all, is extremely rare. Therefore, we are probably living in a dreamworld if we think we can go through life without making judgments about truth or goodness or beauty or worth.

The Bible even goes further and says that not only are we virtually never neutral, but as fallen humans, our will is bent toward the wrong preferences. Our will spontaneously inclines; and it spontaneously inclines wrongly. "The wrath of God is revealed from heaven against all ungodliness and unrighteousness of men, who by their unrighteousness suppress the truth" (Rom. 1:18). By nature, humans, without the transforming grace of God, suppress true judgments. This does not mean that fallen humans cannot calculate that $2 + 2 = 4$. It means that without God's grace such calculations will always confirm Christ-diminishing unbelief. In other words, they may, through the common grace of God, be able to evaluate correctly that $2 + 2 = 4$ is a true calculation, and yet instinctively prefer not to see this as a pointer to the reality of God, much less Christ.

So not only can we not escape the inevitability that we are evaluating creatures; we also cannot escape the reality that we all come into the world with a sinful bent to use our evaluating powers to confirm our rebellion against God. As Paul says in Romans 8:7–8, "The mind of the flesh [that is, the natural human mind, before it is redeemed by Christ] is hostile to God, for it does not submit to God's law; indeed, it cannot." Therefore, as unredeemed sinners, we suppress judgments that honor God, exalt Christ, and lead people to eternal joy (including our own).

So, there are at least three reasons why we should seek to evaluate fairly and correctly. (1) It honors God and his Son. (2) It serves people. (3) It leads to joy.

Correct Evaluation Honors God

The most basic reason why fair and true evaluation honors God is that God is the ultimate standard of all true evaluations. Without God, there would be no such thing as a true evaluation, because there would be no final standard by which anything could be called true. We have seen how essential God is as the foundation of *observation* and *understanding*.

The ultimate reason we can hope to *observe* things accurately is that there is really something outside ourselves to observe. And that is so because God created the world and holds it in being. God and his action in creation are the basis for observation.

Similarly, God is the foundation for all *understanding* because all valid logic is rooted in his character. Trying to make sense out of things without God's underlying existence would be impossible because "making sense" would only be the meaningless movement of matter in our brains if God were not a God of "sense" who gives validity to all "making sense."

So now, when we come to evaluation, the same is true. All valid evaluation is based on the fact that there is an ultimate standard by which things can be assessed as true or false, good or bad, right or wrong, beautiful or ugly, just or unjust. That standard is God. The reason God is the ultimate standard is that there is no standard outside God that did not come from God. When God said to Moses that his name was "I AM WHO I AM" (Ex. 3:14), he meant that there is no other reality before him or outside him that determines what he is like. God is absolute existence. Nothing was there before him. He never came into existence. "From everlasting to everlasting you are God" (Ps. 90:2). He depends on nothing. All that is depends on him. Therefore, there is an objective standard of what is true and good and just and right and beautiful and excellent and precious.

God Is True

It is possible to evaluate things as true because God is true, and He has revealed himself in Christ and in his words which are true. Jesus said, "I am the way, and the *truth*, and the life" (John 14:6). Even his adversaries knew he embodied the truth: "Teacher, we know that you are *true* and teach the way of God truthfully" (Matt. 22:16). Jesus is the truth because he is the incarnate God (John 1:14), and God is "the God of truth" (Isa. 65:16). "Whoever receives [Jesus's] testimony sets his seal to this, that God is true" (John 3:33). "Let God be true though everyone were a liar" (Rom. 3:4).

God's Words Are True

Because God is true, all his words and ways are true. "O Lord GOD, you are God, and your words are true" (2 Sam. 7:28). Indeed, "every word of God proves true" (Prov. 30:5). "Yes, Lord

God the Almighty, true and just are your judgments!" (Rev. 16:7). That is why it is possible to evaluate in the hope that our judgments are not meaningless. They are not mere collisions of molecules in the brains. There is such a reality as truth. It is rooted in God. And he has made his truth known in his word. If we *observe* it and *understand* it correctly, we may have confidence that our *evaluations* based on it are rooted in ultimate reality.

God and His Words Are Good

Similarly, God is the ultimate standard of what is *good*. Evaluations of something as good can have meaning because God is good and the measure of all good. In a provocative statement that was designed to draw all attention away from the human origins of good, including Jesus himself viewed as merely human, Jesus said, "Why do you call me good? No one is good except God alone" (Mark 10:18). If there is any good among men, it is from God, who alone is good.

God is the source and measure of all good. No authority exists outside of God to show him what is good. No one has ever been his counselor, "for from him and through him and to him are all things" (Rom. 11:34, 36). Good comes from inside of him, not outside. Good exists because God exists. "Good and upright is the LORD" (Ps. 25:8). "Oh, taste and see that the LORD is good" (Ps. 34:8). "The LORD is good; his steadfast love endures forever, and his faithfulness to all generations" (Ps. 100:5).

Until sin marred his creation, God pronounced everything good, even very good (Gen. 1:31). He has come into the world in Jesus Christ who redeems people from what is not good. His people, therefore, are called to do good (Gal. 6:9) and to hold fast to what is good (Rom. 12:9). Which means that valid evaluative judgments about what is good are possible. They are grounded in God, who is the measure of all good.

We need not belabor the point with every possible criterion of evaluation. Suffice it to say that all valid evaluative judgments about what is just (Deut. 32:4; Rev. 15:3), what is right (Ps. 19:8; 25:8; 33:4; Hos. 14:9), what is beautiful (Ps. 27:4; Isa. 33:17), what is excellent (1 Pet. 2:9; 2 Pet. 1:3), and what is precious (Job 22:24–25; Ps. 36:7; 139:17; Phil. 3:7–8) are rooted in God. What God is, and what he teaches, is just and right and beautiful and excellent and precious. We can evaluate truly because God is the ground of all value and has revealed himself in his world and his word.

Worship Is (Intensely Positive) Evaluation

Therefore, we say again that the most basic reason why fair and true evaluation honors God is that God is the ultimate standard of all true evaluations. This is not simply a philosophical statement about the ultimate ground of valid evaluations. It also has personal and practical implications for worship—lifelong daily worship, as well as corporate worship with God's people. If God is not the ultimate source and ground of all excellence, then all expressions of worship are meaningless. Jesus said that "God is spirit, and those who worship him must worship in spirit and truth" (John 4:24). But there is no such thing as worship "in truth" if God is not absolute truth. If God is not the truth, there is no truth, and all worship "in truth" ceases.

The same can be said of worshiping "in spirit." Worship consists not simply in speaking truths about God. It consists also in how we evaluate those truths. Worship expresses the *worth* of God. Worship is not the ascription of truths to God that we find boring or repulsive and worthless. Worship is the ascription to God of truths about him that we value. If we do not value them as part of who God is, then we are not worshiping. Worshiping is evaluation. We see God in his word and in his world, and we evaluate him as supremely true and good and beautiful and just and wise and loving and holy, and we say to him and to each other, "I value this God. I value these things about God more than I value anything!" That is what worship is.

Correct Evaluation Serves People

A second reason we should seek to evaluate fairly and correctly is that it serves people. We can't love people if we are indifferent to evaluating correctly. Love presumes that we are seeking to do good for people, but we can't pursue the good if we can't recognize and approve what is good. Therefore, no evaluation, no love.

Paul says, "Let love be genuine. Abhor what is evil; hold fast to what is good" (Rom. 12:9). This means that genuine love cannot be indifferent to what is evil and what is good. To love genuinely, one must be able to evaluate what is evil and good. Again, Paul says, "Love does no wrong to a neighbor" (Rom. 13:10). Therefore, if we cannot tell the difference between right and wrong, we will not be able to choose love.

Again, the apostle says, "[Love] does not rejoice at wrongdoing, but rejoices with the truth" (1 Cor. 13:6). Therefore, if we fail to evaluate correctly and decide what is true and what is wrong, we will not be able to love. Finally, Paul says, "Let our people learn to devote themselves to good works, so as to help cases of urgent need, and not be unfruitful" (Titus 3:14). What, then, if we cannot tell the difference between "good works" and "bad works"? Then we will not be truly helpful in meeting people's real needs. We will not love.

Correct Evaluation Leads to Joy

Not only does correct evaluation honor God and serve people; it also leads to joy—ours and others'. This becomes obvious from Scripture in at least six ways.

First, if we do not evaluate correctly what we observe and understand, we will not be able to know that God is good. And it is precisely the goodness of God that is the ground of all our joy. "Oh, taste and see that the LORD is good! Blessed [happy] is the man who takes refuge in him!" (Ps. 34:8). If we do not evaluate and recognize the goodness of God and fly to him for refuge, we will miss out on full and everlasting joy: "In your presence there is fullness of joy; at your right hand are pleasures forevermore" (Ps. 16:11).

Second, if we do not evaluate correctly what we observe and understand, we will not recognize the gospel for what it is—good news. And if we cannot discern that the gospel is good news, we will not embrace it as our salvation and joy. "Fear not, for behold, I bring you good news of great joy" (Luke 2:10). "How beautiful upon the mountains are the feet of him who brings good news, who publishes peace, who brings good news of happiness" (Isa. 52:7). If we can't evaluate the gospel as good news, we lose the joy of the gospel.

Third, if we do not evaluate correctly what we observe and understand, we will not see the goodness in the promises and purposes of God. But it is the goodness of God's mysterious purposes for us that enables us to rejoice in tribulation (Rom. 5:3). "We know that for those who love God all things work together for good" (Rom. 8:28). "I will make with them an everlasting covenant, that I will not turn away from doing good to them" (Jer. 32:40–41). If we fail to evaluate the purposes and promises of God as good, we lose the basis for experiencing the Christian miracle of "sorrowful, yet always rejoicing" (2 Cor. 6:10).

Fourth, if we fail to evaluate correctly, we will not hunger and thirst for righteousness (Matt. 5:6), and will lose the joy of the upright in heart. "Be glad in the LORD, and rejoice, O righteous, and shout for joy, all you upright in heart!" (Ps. 32:11). "Blessed [happy!] are those who do righteousness at all times!" (Ps. 106:3). "Shout for joy in the LORD, O you righteous! Praise befits the upright" (Ps. 33:1). "Light is sown for the righteous, and joy for the upright in heart" (Ps. 97:11). If we don't evaluate correctly what is right, we will lose the joy of those who pursue it.

Fifth, if we do not evaluate correctly, we will lose the joy that comes from the abundance of God's good gifts. Joy in the goodness of God's gifts assumes we evaluate them as good. "You shall rejoice in all the good that the LORD your God has given to you and to your house" (Deut. 26:11).

Sixth, if we do not evaluate correctly, we will not be a means to the deepest and longest joy of others. We have already seen that we cannot love others if we cannot evaluate what is good for them. Since love means we are willing to sacrifice for the deepest and longest joy of others, therefore, we must be able to evaluate what is good for them if we are to bring them with us into the joy that lasts forever. Everything Jesus spoke and did was designed to bring everlasting joy to everyone who believes (John 3:16; 15:11). Our job is to show that good news of great joy to as many people as we can. But we will never be inclined to share this joy if we do not evaluate the work and words of Jesus as good.

What It Means to Evaluate Fairly

I have tried to show so far in this chapter that the failure to evaluate as we ought is dishonoring to God, irresponsible and unloving in human relationships, and a dead end in our quest for joy (ours and others'). Included in this effort has been the demonstration that God himself, revealed in his world and his word, is the standard by which we evaluate. Now we turn to the word *fairly*. I have said that we should evaluate not only correctly but fairly. What does that mean?

I like to paraphrase the biblical Golden Rule (Matt. 7:12; Luke 6:31) as "Do unto authors as you would have authors do to you." The fundamental principle, then, would be *understand before you criticize*—before you evaluate. Understand before you agree or disagree. That is the way we all would like to be treated. Hear me out before you criticize me. Of course, that principle applies to speakers as well as authors.

Folly and Shame

The most explicit statement of the principle in the Bible is Proverbs 18:13: "If one gives an answer before he hears, it is his folly and shame." Why is it folly to respond before you understand what someone says? Why is it folly to say, "I don't know what you mean, but I disagree with you." This is folly because it's like shooting arrows at what is not there. Tilting at windmills, as they say. In fact, it's even more foolish than shooting at nothing. Actually you are shooting at your own imaginary creation of what you think the author means. The targets of your criticism exist only in your head. You are shooting at yourself.

This kind of criticism before understanding is shameful because it is dishonest. You are claiming to be criticizing the author's ideas. But you are not. You are distorting or ignoring his ideas, then criticizing them, and then claiming to be right. God is not pleased with this kind of dishonest interaction. The shameful habit of criticizing without understanding is probably rooted in the deeper sin of self-exaltation, which is a form of pride. "A fool takes no pleasure in understanding, but only in expressing his opinion" (Prov. 18:2).

This is the folly and shame of pride. We don't want to be shown wrong. And one way of avoiding such exposure is to avoid the dangerous work of understanding. Such understanding might change our mind. Which is humbling. Better, then, to simply dodge the issue of understanding, distort what is said, and exult in our own opinion over the other person's meaning, which in fact may not be what he means.

Mortimer Adler points out that authors are not able to talk to you and say things like, " 'Here, wait till I'm finished, before you start disagreeing.' He cannot protest that the reader has misunderstood him, has missed his point."[1] So, Adler says, "what is important is that there is an *intellectual* etiquette to be observed. Without it, conversation is bickering rather than profitable communication."[2] The main rule in this etiquette (which we have

---

1 Mortimer J. Adler and Charles Van Doren, *How to Read a Book: The Classic Guide to Intelligent Reading* (New York: Touchstone, 1972), 137.
2 Adler and Van Doren, *How to Read a Book*, 138.

seen is a biblical rule, not just a courteous one) is that "you must be able to say, with reasonable certainty, 'I understand,' before you can say any one of the following things: 'I agree,' or 'I disagree,' or 'I suspend judgment.' . . . To agree without understanding is inane. To disagree without understanding is impudent."[3]

Give Reasons for Your Evaluation

Implicit in this rule of fair evaluation (understand before you evaluate) is the rule that we should have reasons for our evaluation. That is the point of understanding. We are reading in order to learn and grow toward greater maturity. We grow not merely by deciding that we agree or disagree, but by seeing reasons for why we agree or disagree. Without seeing reasons, we are not growing in knowledge but only accumulating opinions.

Adler puts it like this: "Respect the difference between knowledge and mere personal opinion, by giving reasons for any critical judgment you make."[4] One of the best pieces of advice I ever received for reading biblical commentaries, for example, is this: Look for the arguments, not the conclusions. Which means: Look for reasons, not opinions.

It is helpful, when thinking about evaluating a book adversely, to ponder the legitimate criticisms one might give of the book's argument. Adler makes this proposal:

The four [ways in which a book may be adversely criticized] can be briefly summarized by conceiving the reader as conversing with the author, as talking back. After he has said, "I under-

3   Adler and Van Doren, *How to Read a Book*, 142–43.
4   Adler and Van Doren, *How to Read a Book*, 150.

stand but I disagree," he can make the following remarks to the author: (1) "You are uninformed;" (2) "You are misinformed;" (3) "You are illogical—your reasoning is not cogent;" (4) "Your analysis is incomplete."[5]

Uninformed: the author did not attend to all the necessary factors.

Misinformed: the author failed to confirm the accuracy of his sources.

Illogical: the author drew inferences from premises that were not logically valid.

Incomplete: the author was selective or careless and did not take into account all the relevant issues.

Of course, one might make stylistic and attitudinal criticisms, but Adler simply is talking about whether the argument for the author's point is compelling. If we evaluate it as not compelling, Adler says, we should be able to give reasons. And those reasons will relate to one or more of these four weaknesses: Uninformed. Misinformed. Illogical. Incomplete.

What about Sin?

As much as I admire Adler's *How to Read a Book*, and appreciate so much of its good advice for fruitful and fair reading, I have to admit that his worldview leaves him with a superficial assessment of the greatest obstacle to fair and correct evaluation. I think he is misinformed. His interpretation of human irrationality overlooks

5   Adler and Van Doren, *How to Read a Book*, 156.

the problem of sin. Why is it that people do not all use their observing and reasoning powers to understand accurately and assess fairly and correctly? Here's his analysis. He is trying to overcome the hopeless skepticism that people just won't agree:

> One is hopeless about the fruitfulness of discussion if he does not recognize that all rational men can agree. Note that we said "can agree." We did not say all rational men *do* agree. Even when they do not agree, they can. . . . These two facts, that people do disagree and can agree, arise from the complexity of human nature. Men are rational animals. Their rationality is the source of their power to agree. Their animality, and the imperfections of their reason that it entails, is the cause of most of the disagreements that occur. Men are creatures of passion and prejudice.[6]

"Men are rational animals." That is the tip-off to the worldview. All we are is rational animals—animals with a higher level of reasoning than the rest of the animals. We do not have souls that are responsible to God and capable of relating to God in joyful submission or proud rebellion. Thus, Adler's assessment of our "passion and prejudice" is that we are the victims of "animality." He has no place for sin, which profoundly corrupts and distorts the way we observe and understand and evaluate. Therefore, his argument for how to read well is not only misinformed about the nature of man (not to mention the blinding effects of Satan) but also incomplete in leaving out the hope of redemption.

6   Adler and Van Doren, *How to Read a Book*, 147.

Biblical Diagnosis and Remedy

What Christian Scripture provides is the profound insight into the reality of sin as a huge obstacle to moving from understanding to evaluation. Here is Paul's description of humans without Christ: "They are darkened in their understanding, alienated from the life of God because of the ignorance that is in them, due to their hardness of heart" (Eph. 4:18). "Although they knew God, they did not honor him as God or give thanks to him, but they became futile in their thinking, and their foolish hearts were darkened" (Rom. 1:21). The corruption and rebellion of sin brings with it darkness. That is, we do not understand or evaluate in the light of God's reality. Therefore, we turn reality upside down: "Their god is their belly, and they glory in their shame" (Phil. 3:19). In other words, fully correct evaluation becomes impossible without redemption.

Justification and Right Evaluation

But Scripture also provides us a way out of this blindness and darkness. At the root of our blinding corruption is real guilt before God. Christ came into the world and died to bear the punishment for that guilt (Rom. 8:3). He became a curse for us (Gal. 3:13). He bore our sins in his body (1 Pet. 3:25). He was pierced for our transgressions (Isa. 53:5). The wrath of God's justice was satisfied (Rom. 3:25). Therefore, when we trust Christ as our treasured Savior and Lord, our sins are forgiven. "Everyone who believes in him receives forgiveness of sins through his name" (Acts 10:43). United to him by faith (Gal. 3:26), we are justified before God (Rom. 5:1). We are adopted as God's sons (Gal. 4:5).

The Holy Spirit is poured out into our hearts (Rom. 5:5). And we are transferred from the domain of darkness to the kingdom of Christ (Col. 1:13).

Sanctification and Right Evaluation

Now begins a lifetime of transformation from one degree of glory to the next (2 Cor. 3:18). Jesus says, "I am the light of the world. Whoever follows me will not walk in darkness, but will have the light of life" (John 8:12). We are "called . . . out of darkness into his marvelous light" (1 Pet. 2:9). "God has shone in our hearts to give the light of the knowledge of the glory of God in the face of Jesus Christ" (2 Cor. 4:6). "At one time you were darkness, but now you are light in the Lord. Walk as children of light" (Eph. 5:8).

By the sin-forgiving power of Christ's justification, and by the sin-conquering power of the Spirit's transformation, Satan's reason-ruining bondage in our lives is broken so that we "come to [our] senses and escape from the snare of the devil, after being captured by him to do his will" (2 Tim. 2:26). The eyes of our heart are enlightened (Eph. 1:18), and we begin to see reality the way it really is. We begin to grow in our ability to evaluate fairly and correctly. The cross of Christ ceases to be foolishness and a stumbling block (1 Cor. 1:23–24).

Necessity of Prayer

As we have seen with the habits of observation and understanding, prayer is essential in the task of lifelong learning. When Paul prayed "that your love may abound more and more, with knowledge and all discernment," he followed this with the aim of this discernment: "so that you may approve what is excellent"

(Phil. 1:9–10). That is, so that you may evaluate correctly. Clearly prayer is essential—that is, God's help is essential—for redeemed sinners to grow in their ability to evaluate fairly and correctly.

Lifetime of Growth in Evaluation

Lifelong learning means growing in the habit of mind and heart that seeks not only to *observe* carefully and thoroughly, and to *understand* accurately, but also to *evaluate* fairly and correctly. We have seen that evaluation is inevitable. Our wills do this automatically. But doing it fairly and correctly is not automatic. This is the challenge of a lifetime. This is what lifelong learning is for.

4

Feeling

*We want to grow for a lifetime in our capacity
to feel properly what we have observed
and understood and evaluated.*

LIFELONG EDUCATION SHOULD seek to form the heart with its
feelings as well as the mind with its ideas. I recognize that changing
someone's mind and changing someone's heart are very different
tasks. Someone's ideas may be changed by compelling arguments,
but the feelings of the heart do not respond in the same way. They
are more spontaneous and do not lie in the immediate control
even of those who have them. For example, seldom is anyone
argued out of anger or grief. Understanding lifelong education
as the formation of the heart with its feelings makes clear that
the task of education is not merely human but involves the work
of God's Spirit.

Feelings Are Essential

Feelings are not marginal in the making of an emotionally healthy and mature person. In fact, there is no human wholeness where these three realities are not present: the *feelings* of the heart, the *thoughts* of the mind, and the *decisions* of the will. Someone is not complete in his education if his thoughts are true and his decisions are moral, but his feelings are misdirected, disproportionate, or dead.

By *misdirected*, I mean that he may desire to have illicit sex, or may fear stepping on the cracks in the sidewalk, or may love money. By *disproportionate*, I mean that he may love his cat more than his neighbor, or may feel more fear of human criticism than of displeasing God, or may feel more anger at his wife's sins than his own. By *dead* feelings, I mean that a person may lose a loved one, or see a horrible car accident, or deeply hurt another person, and yet feel nothing. In other words, if education aims at whole persons, it cannot be indifferent to the formation of the heart and its feelings.

Why Feelings Matter

Even non-Christians agree that feelings can be misdirected, disproportionate, or dead. And most non-Christians would agree that some efforts should be made along the way to pursue emotional health. But the Christian view of human feelings goes beyond the merely human perspective that does not account for the everlasting human soul and the reality of God. For Christians, far more is at stake than a common view of emotional health that enables a person to get along in this world.

The Bible puts a huge emphasis on the human heart with its feelings. And it does so not mainly because proper feelings enable a person to get along in this world, but mainly because they are permanently satisfying to the human soul, and are essential to glorifying God and loving people. The lifelong education we pursue aims at eternally happy persons who love people and glorify God. All three of these aims can be attained only by a formation of the heart that is growing in its authentic experience of living feelings that are directed toward fitting objects in proportion to the nature of those objects.

What Are Feelings?

Before I show the prominence of human feelings in the Bible, and why this is the case, let's take a moment to define what we mean by "feelings." The word *feeling* can refer to a wide array of human experiences. It can refer to the sensitivity of the skin. For example, we might say, "Do you have any feeling in your big toe?" Or it might refer to the physical aspects of emotion. For example, we might say before we give a public speech, "I feel butterflies in my stomach," meaning that the emotional feelings of anxiety are detectable in the body. In my view, the more one focuses on the merely physical aspect of "feelings," the less significant they become morally and spiritually. That is not our focus here.

What we are most concerned about is the aspects of "feeling" that are owing to the condition of the heart and reveal its true moral condition. Jesus says, "From within, out of the heart of man, come . . . sensuality, envy . . . pride, foolishness. All these evil things come from within, and they defile a person" (Mark 7:21–23). Of course, we may speak of evil *deeds* coming from the heart. I omitted those in the verses just quoted simply to focus on the fact that feelings too come from the heart, and they can be evil.

In another place Jesus says, "Woe to you, scribes and Pharisees, hypocrites! For you clean the outside of the cup and the plate, but inside they are full of greed and self-indulgence" (Matt. 23:25–26). That's another way of saying that the heart is the source of the sinful feelings of greed and self-indulgence. James located the source of outward conflict in the feelings of the heart: "What causes quarrels and what causes fights among you? Is it not this, that your *passions* are at war within you? You *desire* and do not have, so you murder. You *covet* and cannot obtain, so you fight and quarrel" (James 4:1–2). Passions. Desires. Covetousness. They are evil in themselves. And they cause much outward sin.

My concern with feelings is with these morally significant feelings, not with the more physical aspects of feeling. We don't think of big toes that have no feeling as being morally evil. But we do think of sensuality and envy and pride as evil. That is our concern. Feelings that are evil and need to be changed, and feelings that are good and need to grow.

What Does It Mean to Call a Feeling Good?

Referring to feelings as "good" calls for another clarification. Because of common grace—God's nonsaving but gracious gifts to the unbelieving world (Matt. 5:45; Acts 14:17; Rom. 2:4)—non-Christians can have "good" feelings. They are "good" in the sense that their feelings enable life to be lived with some measure of relational peace and personal pleasure and the public acknowledgment of maturity and health. But in another sense, these "good" feelings are not good in relation to God. They are not consciously God-honoring. They don't come from a heart of faith.

Even the most mature and balanced feelings in unbelievers are not growing in the soil of faith. They do not come from a heart that is trusting in the grace of God in Christ for the producing of the fruit of the Holy Spirit—"love, joy, peace, patience, kindness, goodness, faithfulness, gentleness, self-control" (Gal. 5:22–23). Their feelings are not shaped by the Holy Spirit. They don't have the form and fragrance of Christ (Rom. 8:29; Gal. 4:19). Nor do they proceed from the heart with the hope and desire that God would be glorified through them. They are not from Christ, or through Christ, or for Christ. They are not "from faith"—and Paul said that "whatever does not proceed from faith is sin" (Rom. 14:23).

Our concern with lifelong education focuses on the pursuit of feelings that are "from faith." I call these *spiritual affections*. They are *affections* in the sense that they are feelings that have moral significance as coming from the heart (not merely the body). And they are *spiritual* in the sense that they are caused, shaped, and directed by the Holy Spirit through faith.

Importance of Feelings in the Bible

Now, with these clarifications, we turn to the prevalence and importance of feelings in the Bible. First, take a glimpse at the range of the feelings expressed in the psalms. This is surely one of the reasons the psalms are so deeply loved by so many Christians. They give expression to an amazing array of human feelings. Here is a sample:

- Loneliness: "I am *lonely* and afflicted" (Ps. 25:16).
- Love: "I *love* you, O LORD, my strength" (Ps. 18:1).

- Awe: "Let all the inhabitants of the world stand in *awe* of him" (Ps. 33:8).
- Sorrow: "My life is spent with *sorrow*" (Ps. 31:10).
- Regret: "I am *sorry* for my sin" (Ps. 38:18).
- Contrition: "A broken and *contrite* heart, O God, you will not despise" (Ps. 51:17).
- Discouragement: "Why are you *cast down*, O my soul?" (Ps. 42:5).
- Turmoil: "O my soul, why are you *in turmoil* within me?" (Ps. 42:5).
- Shame: "*Shame* has covered my face" (Ps. 44:15).
- Exultation: "In your salvation how greatly he *exults*" (Ps. 21:1).
- Marveling: "This is the LORD's doing; it is *marvelous* in our eyes" (Ps. 118:23).
- Delight: "His *delight* is in the law of the LORD" (Ps. 1:2).
- Joy: "You have put more *joy* in my heart than they have when their grain and wine abound" (Ps. 4:7).
- Gladness: "I will *be glad* and exult in you" (Ps. 9:2).
- Fear: "Serve the LORD with *fear*" (Ps. 2:11).
- Anger: "Be *angry*, and do not sin" (Ps. 4:4).
- Peace: "In *peace* I will both lie down and sleep" (Ps. 4:8).
- Grief: "My eye wastes away because of *grief*" (Ps. 6:7).
- Desire: "O LORD, you hear the *desire* of the afflicted" (Ps. 10:17).
- Hope: "Let your steadfast love, O LORD, be upon us, even as we *hope* in you" (Ps. 33:22).
- Brokenheartedness: "The LORD is near to the *brokenhearted* and saves the crushed in spirit" (Ps. 34:18).

- Thankfulness: "I will *thank* you in the great congregation" (Ps. 35:18).
- Zeal: "*Zeal* for your house has consumed me" (Ps. 69:9).
- Pain: "I am afflicted and in *pain*" (Ps. 69:29).
- Confidence: "Though war arise against me, yet I will be *confident*" (Ps. 27:3).

From such a list, we are able to conclude that feelings are not marginal to the spiritual maturity and health of the Christian. They are a huge part of human experience and belong to the essence, not the margins, of what it means to be a godly person.

Right Feelings Not Optional

But more important than the prevalence and array of feelings is the explicit teaching in many texts of the New Testament that spiritual affections are essential, not optional, to being a Christian. Here is a sampling of such feelings that God calls us to have—feelings that are our *duty*. We *should* have these feelings.

Christians should feel *joy*:

Rejoice in the Lord always; again I will say, *rejoice*. (Phil. 4:4)

Christians should feel *contentment* in their hearts:

Keep your life free from love of money, and be *content* with what you have, for he has said, "I will never leave you nor forsake you." (Heb. 13:5)

Christian should feel fervent *brotherly love* from the heart:

> Having purified your souls by your obedience to the truth for a sincere *brotherly love*, love one another earnestly from a pure heart. (1 Pet. 1:22)

Christians should feel *hope*:

> Therefore, preparing your minds for action, and being sober-minded, set your *hope* fully on the grace that will be brought to you at the revelation of Jesus Christ. (1 Pet. 1:13)

Christians should feel *fear* of God, not of persecutors:

> I will warn you whom to *fear*: fear him who, after he has killed, has authority to cast into hell. Yes, I tell you, *fear* him! (Luke 12:5)

Christians should feel *peace*:

> Let the *peace* of Christ rule in your hearts. (Col. 3:15)

Christians should feel *zeal* and *fervency*:

> Do not be slothful in *zeal*, be *fervent* in spirit. (Rom. 12:11)

Christians should feel *sorrow* with the sorrowful:

> Rejoice with those who rejoice, and *weep* with those who weep. (Rom. 12:15)

Christians should feel *longing* for God's word:

> Like newborn infants, *long for* the pure spiritual milk. (1 Pet. 2:2)

Christians should feel *tenderheartedness*:

> Be kind to one another, *tenderhearted*, forgiving one another, as God in Christ forgave you. (Eph. 4:32)

Christians should feel *thankful*:

> Be filled with the Spirit . . . making melody to the Lord with *your heart*, *giving thanks* always and for everything to God the Father in the name of our Lord Jesus Christ. (Eph. 5:19–20)

Christians should feel a sense of *lowliness*:

> Do nothing from selfish ambition or conceit, but in *humility* [lowliness] count others more significant than yourselves. (Phil. 2:3)

Christians should feel *sympathy*:

> All of you, have unity of mind, *sympathy*, brotherly love, a tender heart, and a humble mind. (1 Pet. 3:8)

Christians should feel *brotherly affection*:

> Love one another with *brotherly affection*. (Rom. 12:10)

In view of texts like these, we can conclude that feelings—spiritual affections—are not peripheral or optional to the Christian life. They are at the heart of what it means to be a new creature in Christ. The ongoing life of a Christian includes the daily act of faith by which we "put off [our] old self, which . . . is corrupt through deceitful *desires* . . . and . . . put on the new self, created after the likeness of God in true righteousness and holiness" (Eph. 4:22–24). We are commanded to "put off" or "put to death" feelings like passion, evil desire, covetousness (Col. 3:5), anxiety (Matt. 6:25), anger (Matt. 5:22), bitterness (Eph. 4:31), lust (Matt. 5:28), greed (1 Cor. 5:11), and worldly grief (2 Cor. 7:10). The old self was ruined by "deceitful *desires*," and the new self is being transformed with holy desires. This is the work of the Holy Spirit (Gal. 5:22–23).

Now the question is, Why has God made spiritual affections so central to human existence? I pointed to the answer earlier when I said that such feelings are permanently satisfying to the human soul, and that they are essential to glorifying God and loving people.

God Aims at Happy People

The clearest example of a well-directed, proportionate, living feeling is the feeling of wholehearted happiness in God himself. The coming into being of this spiritual affection is the breath of eternal life, the sign of new birth. When the human soul discovers God himself as the blazing sun of satisfaction at the center of the solar system of our life, then all the planets of our other affections and behaviors begin to find their God-appointed orbits. To have God as the supreme satisfaction of our souls is the living force that begins to bring all other desires into proper direction and proper proportion.

The obvious message of the whole Bible is that God intends to make his people supremely happy in his own presence forever. This happiness is the sum of all spiritual affections. From the times of the Old Testament, God's purpose was the happiness of his people.

> The ransomed of the LORD shall return
>> and come to Zion with *singing*;
> everlasting *joy* shall be upon their heads;
>> they shall obtain *gladness* and *joy*,
>> and sorrow and sighing shall flee away. (Isa. 35:10)

Jesus came into the world bringing "good news of *great joy*" (Luke 2:10). His message had been set for him from of old. It was "good news of happiness."

> How beautiful upon the mountains
>> are the feet of him who brings good news,
> who publishes peace, who brings good news of *happiness*,
>> who publishes salvation,
>> who says to Zion, "Your God reigns." (Isa. 52:7)

Jesus told Pilate why he had come into the world: "For this purpose I was born and for this purpose I have come into the world— to bear witness to the truth" (John 18:37). And he explained to his disciples that when he spoke the words of this truth, he did so for their joy: "These things I have spoken to you, that my *joy* may be in you, and that your *joy* may be full" (John 15:11; cf. 17:13).

The apostle Peter explains why Jesus died. It was to bring us to God and joy. He says, "Christ also suffered once for sins, the righteous for the unrighteous, that he might bring us to God" (1 Pet. 3:18). And what do we experience when we find ourselves in the presence of God with Christ? "Though you have not seen him, you love him. . . . You . . . rejoice with joy that is inexpressible and filled with glory" (1 Pet. 1:8). Coming to God is coming to joy: "In your presence there is fullness of *joy*; at your right hand are *pleasures* forevermore" (Ps. 16:11). That is God's eternal plan.

Therefore, joy is not optional in the Christian life. We were destined for this. God commands it repeatedly. "*Rejoice* in the Lord" (Phil. 3:1). "*Be glad* in the Lord" (Ps. 32:11). "Shout for *joy* in the Lord" (Ps. 33:1). "Let all the upright in heart *exult*" (Ps. 64:10). And he commands that we serve him with joy, not with a gloomy sense of obligation: "Serve the Lord with *gladness*!" (Ps. 100:2). "Give . . . not reluctantly or under compulsion, for God loves a *cheerful* giver" (2 Cor. 9:7). "The one who does acts of mercy, [let him do it] with *cheerfulness*" (Rom. 12:8). So I conclude that one of the reasons God has made spiritual affections essential to Christian existence is that his gracious aim from all eternity was to have a happy people for himself.

Happiness in God for God

It gets even better. God's aim in creating the universe was not only for our happiness, but also for his glory.

> Bring my sons from afar
> and my daughters from the end of the earth,

everyone who is called by my name,
    whom I created for *my glory*. (Isa. 43:6–7)

That is, God aimed to communicate his glory to his creation so that we might see it and be glad in it. In creation, he intended that his glory be magnified and our souls be satisfied. And the relationship between these two aims fills us with wonder and gives a special passion to our pursuit of lifelong learning.

Most Bible-saturated Christians recognize that God has this double purpose in creation—his glory and our joy. It has been enshrined in the familiar first question of the Westminster Catechism: What is man's chief end? Answer: Man's chief end is to glorify God and enjoy him forever. God's glory and our joy are the double aim of creation. But it is surprising how few Christians see the relationship between these two. Yet it has thrilling implications. It is this relationship between our joy and God's glory that energizes us for the task of lifelong learning.

Our Chief End: Glorify God *by* Enjoying Him Forever

The relationship is that enjoyment of God is one way that we glorify God. *God is most glorified in us when we are most satisfied in him.* I call this Christian Hedonism. These are not simply two unrelated goals alongside each other. God has designed the world so that our joy in him would be the way the worth of his glory shines. Glorifying God and enjoying God are not distinct pursuits. Enjoying God *is* glorifying God. When you enjoy something supremely, you show that for you it has supreme value. To clarify: I am not merely saying that acts that glorify God should be enjoyable to us. I am saying that enjoying God is one of those acts that glorifies God.

I have argued for this and explained it in the introduction (pp. 4–6). The implication of this wonderful discovery—that God is most glorified in us when we are most satisfied in him—is that the pursuit of our longest and deepest joy is not just permitted, but is required. Pursuing our fullest and most durable happiness in God is our duty, not only because it is commanded in God's word, but also because without it, we do not glorify God as we ought. Which means that the great battle of lifelong education is the battle to be more satisfied in God than in all this world has to offer. Or, as we saw in the introduction (pp. 6–7), the great challenge of lifelong education is to enjoy God *above* and *in* all other legitimate joys. God is the joy *above* all joys. And he is tasted as the best joy *in* all other worthy joys.

Happiness in God and Love for Others

There is one more step to take in explaining why God ordained that feelings—spiritual affections—be essential to human existence. It is feelings—specifically the feeling of joy in God—that makes it possible to love other people. Loving people means sincerely wanting their good and acting as far as we can to pursue it. What we have seen is that the greatest good is to know and enjoy God to the full and forever. "In your presence there is *fullness* of joy; at your right hand are pleasures *forevermore*" (Ps. 16:11). No greater good can be conceived than "full" and "forever." Nothing is fuller than full. Nothing is longer than forever.

Therefore, to love is to seek, whatever the cost, to expand our joy in God so as to include others in it. One reason Jesus says, "It is more blessed to give than to receive" (Acts 20:35), is that in giving our joy in God to others, we experience more of it ourselves. In fact, the reason our pursuit of joy in God is not selfishness is that we do not seek our joy at the expense of others, but rather by including others in it. Nobody calls people selfish if what makes them happy is the enlarging of their joy by sharing it with others—especially if it costs the lover his life, which it often has.

There is a beautiful picture of how this works in 2 Corinthians 8:1–2. We saw this in the introduction, but it is worth rehearsing again. Paul was collecting funds for the poor in Jerusalem (Rom. 15:26). In 2 Corinthians 8, he gives the Macedonian Christians as a model of generosity for the Corinthian Christians to follow. He says, "We want you to know, brothers, about the grace of God that has been given among the churches of Macedonia, for in a severe test of affliction, *their abundance of joy* and their extreme poverty have *overflowed in a wealth of generosity* on their part" (vv. 1–2). The grace of God filled the Macedonian Christians with joy in the midst of affliction and poverty. The effect of this fullness of joy in God's grace was that it "overflowed" in generosity for the poor saints in Jerusalem. A few verses later, in verse 8, Paul calls this kind of generosity "love."

I conclude, therefore, that love is the overflow of joy in God that gladly meets the needs of others. Or, to say it another way, love is the outward impulse of joy in God that seeks to expand itself by including others in it.

I hope it is evident now why God designed that *feelings* be essential to human existence. When rightly directed and proportionate to the beauty and worth of God himself, they give us permanent and profound satisfaction. And they are essential to glorifying God and loving people. Therefore, it is necessary that lifelong education seek to form the heart with its feelings as well as the mind with its ideas.

Pursue Joy

How then shall we pursue the shaping of our hearts and their feelings? In a sense, that question is what this whole book is about. The aim of lifelong learning, and the aim of this book, is mature, emotionally healthy persons whose lives are fruitful in loving people and glorifying God. I hope this book sets you on such a lifelong trajectory. That's what the six habits of heart and mind are for.

But I think it will be helpful if we conclude this chapter with fifteen pointers in the pursuit of soul-satisfying, Christ-exalting, people-loving, God-glorifying feelings. Specifically, since God-glorifying joy is God's goal in creation, the focus of these pointers is just that: How shall we grow in our capacity to feel such joy in every circumstance of life?[1]

1. Realize that authentic joy, and every other spiritual affection, is a gift of God that we don't deserve:

The fruit of the Spirit is . . . joy. (Gal. 5:22)

May the God of peace . . . equip you with everything good that you may do his will, working in us that which is pleasing in

---

1 These pointers correspond to the content of my book *When I Don't Desire God: How to Fight for Joy* (Wheaton, IL: Crossway, 2013).

his sight, through Jesus Christ, to whom be glory forever and ever. Amen. (Heb. 13:21)

2. Realize that joy must be fought for relentlessly (which is not a contradiction of number 1):

Not that we lord it over your faith, but we work with you for your joy. (2 Cor. 1:24)

Fight the good fight of faith. (1 Tim. 6:12)

I have fought the good fight, I finished the course, I have kept the faith. (2 Tim. 4:7)

3. Resolve to attack all known sin in your life:

If you live according to the flesh you will die, but if by the Spirit you put to death the deeds of the body, you will live. (Rom. 8:13)

4. Learn the secret of "gutsy guilt"—how to fight for joy like a justified sinner:

Rejoice not over me, O my enemy;
    when I fall, I shall rise;
when I sit in darkness,
    the Lord will be a light to me.
I will bear the indignation of the Lord
    because I have sinned against him,
until he pleads my cause

and executes judgment for me.
He will bring me out to the light;
    I shall look upon his vindication. (Mic. 7:8–9)

Since we have been justified by faith, we have peace with God
through our Lord Jesus Christ. (Rom. 5:1)

Here is a man who is guilty: "I have sinned against [the Lord]."
But he is so bold as to say that the very Lord whom he has sinned
against will plead his cause and execute judgment "for him," not
against him. That is what I mean by gutsy guilt.

5. Realize that the battle is primarily a fight to see God for who he is:

Taste and see that the LORD is good. (Ps. 34:8)

We all with unveiled face beholding the glory of the Lord are
being changed from one degree of glory to the next. (2 Cor. 3:18)

Beloved we are God's children now, but it does not yet appear
what we shall be, but we know that when he appears we shall
be like him because we shall see him as he is. (1 John 3:1–2)

6. Meditate daily on the word of God:

His delight is in the law of the LORD,
    and on his law he meditates day and night.
He is like a tree
    planted by streams of water

that yields its fruit in its season,
    and its leaf does not wither.
In all that he does, he prospers. (Ps. 1:2–3)

The precepts of the LORD are right,
    rejoicing the heart. (Ps. 19:8)

Your words were found and I ate them,
    and your words became to me a joy
    and the delight of my heart. (Jer. 15:16)

I have spoken these things to you that my joy may be in you
and that your joy may be full. (John 15:11)

7. Pray earnestly and often for open heart-eyes and a heart that
inclines to God:

Open my eyes, that I may behold
    wondrous things out of your law. (Ps. 119:18)

Ask, and it will be given to you; seek, and you will find; knock,
and it will be opened to you. (Matt. 7:7)

I do not cease to give thanks for you, remembering you in my
prayers, that . . . the eyes of your hearts [be] enlightened, that
you may know what is the hope to which he has called you,
what are the riches of his glorious inheritance in the saints, and
what is the immeasurable greatness of his power toward us who
believe. (Eph. 1:16–18)

8. Learn to preach to yourself rather than listen to yourself:

> Why are you cast down, O my soul,
>   and why are you in turmoil within me?
> Hope in God; for I shall again praise him,
>   my salvation and my God. (Ps. 42:5)

9. Spend time with God-saturated people who help you see God and fight for joy:

> Jonathan, Saul's son, rose and went to David at Horesh, and strengthened his hand in God. (1 Sam. 23:16)

> Bad company ruins good morals. (1 Cor. 15:33)

> Exhort one another every day, as long as it is called "today," that none of you may be hardened by the deceitfulness of sin. (Heb. 3:13)

> Let us consider how to stir up one another to love and good works, not neglecting to meet together, as is the habit of some, but encouraging one another, and all the more as you see the Day drawing near. (Heb. 10:24–25)

10. Be patient in the night of God's seeming absence:

> I waited patiently for the LORD;
>   he inclined to me and heard my cry.
> He drew me up from the pit of destruction,

out of the miry bog,
and set my feet upon a rock,
    making my steps secure.
He put a new song in my mouth,
    a song of praise to our God.
Many will see and fear,
    and put their trust in the Lord. (Ps. 40:1–3)

If I say, "Surely the darkness shall cover me,
    and the light about me be night,"
even the darkness is not dark to you;
    the night is bright as the day,
    for darkness is as light with you. (Ps. 139:11–12)

11. Get the rest, exercise, and proper diet that God designed your body to have:

Unless the Lord builds the house,
    those who build it labor in vain.
Unless the Lord watches over the city,
    the watchman stays awake in vain.
It is in vain that you rise up early
    and go late to rest,
eating the bread of anxious toil;
    for he gives to his beloved sleep. (Ps. 127:1–2)

"All things are lawful for me," but not all things are helpful. "All things are lawful for me," but I will not be dominated by anything. "Food is meant for the stomach and the stomach for food"—and

God will destroy both one and the other. The body is not meant for sexual immorality, but for the Lord, and the Lord for the body. (1 Cor. 6:12–13)

I discipline my body and keep it under control, lest after preaching to others I myself should be disqualified. (1 Cor. 9:27)

12. Make use of God's revelation in nature:

The heavens declare the glory of God,
    and the sky above proclaims his handiwork.
Day to day pours out speech,
    and night to night reveals knowledge. . . .
In them he has set a tent for the sun,
which comes out like a bridegroom leaving his chamber,
    and, like a strong man, runs its course with joy.
        (Ps. 19:1–5)

Look at the birds of the air: they neither sow nor reap nor gather into barns, and yet your heavenly Father feeds them. Are you not of more value than they? . . . Consider the lilies of the field, how they grow: they neither toil nor spin, yet I tell you, even Solomon in all his glory was not arrayed like one of these. But if God so clothes the grass of the field, which today is alive and tomorrow is thrown into the oven, will he not much more clothe you, O you of little faith? (Matt. 6:26–30)

13. Read great books about God and biographies of faithful Christians:

[Christ] gave . . . teachers, to equip the saints for the work of ministry, for building up the body of Christ. (Eph. 4:11–12)

Through his faith, though he died, he still speaks. (Heb. 11:4)

Since we are surrounded by so great a cloud of witnesses, let us also lay aside every weight, and sin which clings so closely, and let us run with endurance the race that is set before us. (Heb. 12:1)

Remember your leaders, those who spoke to you the word of God. Consider the outcome of their way of life, and imitate their faith. (Heb. 13:7)

14. Put what you know into practice for the good of others:

Is not this the fast that I choose:
   to loose the bonds of wickedness,
   to undo the straps of the yoke,
to let the oppressed go free,
   and to break every yoke?
Is it not to share your bread with the hungry
   and bring the homeless poor into your house;
when you see the naked, to cover him,
   and not to hide yourself from your own flesh?
Then shall your light break forth like the dawn,
   and your healing shall spring up speedily. (Isa. 58:6–8)

It is more blessed to give than to receive. (Acts 20:35)

15. Get a global vision for the cause of Christ and pour yourself out for the unreached:

> May God be gracious to us and bless us
>> and make his face to shine upon us,
> that your way may be known on earth,
>> your saving power *among all nations.*
> Let *the peoples* praise you, O God;
>> let all the peoples praise you!
>
> Let the nations be glad and sing for joy,
>> for you judge *the peoples* with equity
>> and guide the nations upon earth.
> Let *the peoples* praise you, O God;
>> let *all the peoples* praise you!
>
> The earth has yielded its increase;
>> God, our God, shall bless us.
> God shall bless us;
>> let *all the ends of the earth* fear him! (Ps. 67)

On Our Way to Education

We now have seen four of the six habits of heart and mind: observation, understanding, evaluation, and feeling. One of the aims of lifelong learning is to become the kind of observers and thinkers and evaluators whose hearts respond with feelings that are well-directed, proportionate, and full of life.

God himself is the primary reality to be observed in all observation. He is the ground of all right understanding. His worth and will are the standard of all evaluation. Therefore, he is the source of supreme satisfaction. When he holds that supreme position as the sun in the solar system of our affections, all the other planets move toward their God-designed orbit. We are well on our way to be a properly educated people.

5

Application

*We want to grow for a lifetime in our ability to
apply wisely and helpfully what we have observed
and understood and evaluated and felt.*

OUR QUEST FOR LIFELONG LEARNING includes the effort to
apply what we have observed, understood, evaluated, and felt.
What do we mean by *application*?

It would be possible to think of application as focused on more
observation, understanding, evaluation, and feeling. In other words,
I might say, "I'm going to now take all I've learned so far and apply
it to a new area of learning. So, all I have observed will help me
observe better in this new area. And all I have understood will help
me understand more. And my powers of evaluation and feeling will
make me better at evaluating and feeling in this new field of study."
That would be true and legitimate. All true learning enables more
learning. But that is not what I mean in this chapter by "application."

What I mean is turning our observation, understanding, evaluation, and feeling into action for the sake the glory of God and the good of others. Of course, no matter what we do, we are always learning. But that is not my focus when I speak of the habit of heart and mind called "application." Here we are focusing on the habit of taking what we have learned and seeking ways to turn it into wise and useful action.

Can Joy Have Intentions?

I am aware that, at first, there appears to be a problem if we speak about applying our feelings—that is, turning our feelings into action. The reason this seems like a problem is that authentic feelings are an end in themselves. In the very moment of true feelings, they are not being performed as means to an end. I don't decide to feel fear at the onrushing bear so that I will have strength to run. I don't feel ecstasy in the arms of my wife so that the argument between us will be resolved. I don't feel the sweetness of Jesus's presence in worship so that he will heal my child. I don't feel thankful for a precious gift so that my children will learn gratitude. I don't feel anger at the murder of the innocent person so that law enforcement will do its job. I don't feel desire for food so that the preparation will go faster.

Authentic feelings are not like that. In the moment when they are being felt, they are not purposeful decisions. Premeditated decisions are a conscious means of pursuing some end beyond themselves. I decide to shoot the bear. I decide to speak to my wife about the conflict. I decide to pray earnestly for the healing of my child. I decide to teach my children the importance of gratitude. I decide to advocate for just law enforcement. I decide to lend a hand in the kitchen. Decisions work like that. But not feelings. As soon as I try to stand outside the moment of my emotion and make it a means of some other end, the authenticity of my feeling ceases.

So what does it mean to say that the habit of application turns not only observation, understanding, and evaluation, but also feelings, into wise and helpful actions? The solution to this apparent obstacle is found in what we said in the previous chapter about the nature of Christian joy in God. We saw that joy in God has in it an expansive impulse to enlarge itself by including others in it. In one sense, the authentic enjoyment of God is an end in itself. The experience of pleasure in God is not looking beyond God for other ends. God is the end. Nevertheless, God's grace is of such a nature that while sin and futility and suffering and lostness exist in the world, the enjoyment of God will bring with it the desire that our enjoyment overflow to meet the needs of others—to bring them into enjoyment of what God offers to be for them in Christ.

While we live in a fallen world, Christian contentment in God will always be a kind of dissatisfied contentment. This is not because God is deficient as a source of contentment. It is because God himself is the kind of God whose love is expansive. It moves out toward need. This is a mark of its overflowing fullness, not its defect. And when we see this divine love, and are caught up into it as our supreme joy, the very nature of God's love means that our joy in it will share the expansiveness of it.

God is truly the *end* of our quest. He is not a stepping stone to some greater pleasure. But being the kind of gracious God that he is, our contentment in him moves us toward need—not to gain something besides God, but to enjoy fully the kind of need-meeting God that he is. Our joy in him is like a high-pressure weather system which, when it nears a low-pressure system of human need, creates a wind that expands to fill the need. That wind is called *love*.

Application Is Action

With that clarification of how feeling moves toward the application of love, we can state again the fifth habit of lifelong learning: our habit should be to turn our observation, understanding, evaluation, and feeling into wise and helpful action. By wise and helpful action, we mean action for the glory of God and the good of others.

This habit of application in action is reinforced by the relentless thrust of Scripture to turn learning into doing. Repeatedly we see that knowing is for the sake of acting. "Be doers of the word, and not hearers only" (James 1:22). "Let us not love in word or talk but in deed and in truth" (1 John 3:18). "If you know these things, blessed are you if you do them" (John 13:17). "Why do you call me 'Lord, Lord,' and not do what I tell you?" (Luke 6:46). "What good is it, my brothers, if someone says he has faith but does not have works?" (James 2:14). "Everyone then who hears these words of mine and does them will be like a wise man who built his house on the rock" (Matt. 7:24).

Application as Overflow of Joy in God

As I have tried to show, this thrust of Scripture from *knowing* to *doing* is rooted in the nature of Christian love as the overflow of joy in God. We saw one illustration of this in the previous chapter from 2 Corinthians 8:1–2. The Macedonian Christians were an example of love (v. 8) because "in a severe test of affliction, *their abundance of joy* and their extreme poverty have *overflowed in a wealth of generosity.*" The feeling of joy produced the action of generous giving. Paul calls this *love.* The nature of Christian joy is that it gladly overflows to meet the needs of others. That is, it overflows in good deeds. This is what we mean by *application.*

Another illustration of how joy produces a specific application of love is found in Hebrews 12:1–2:

> Since we are surrounded by so great a cloud of witnesses, let us also lay aside every weight, and sin which clings so closely, and let us run with endurance the race that is set before us, looking to Jesus, the founder and perfecter of our faith, who for the joy that was set before him endured the cross, despising the shame, and is seated at the right hand of the throne of God.

Christ was so sure of joy (with his Father and his redeemed people) on the other side of the cross that he could taste enough of it to carry him through the agony of crucifixion. "For the joy that was set before him [he] endured the cross." Which means that the greatest deed of love that has ever been performed was the fruit of joy—even on the path of agony. If there ever was a glorious application of the expansive impulse of joy, it was the cross of Christ.

The writer of Hebrews intends for us to see in Christ's motivation a model for how we turn the feeling of joy into acts of love. For example, Hebrews 10:32–34:

> Recall the former days when, after you were enlightened, you endured a hard struggle with sufferings, sometimes being

publicly exposed to reproach and affliction, and sometimes
being partners with those so treated. For you had compassion
on those in prison, and you joyfully accepted the plundering of
your property, since you knew that you yourselves had a better
possession and an abiding one.

Some Christians had gone to prison for their faith. Those
outside faced a choice. How shall they *apply* what they see and
understand and evaluate and feel? Shall they go underground and
avoid persecution? Or shall they go to the prison and provide for
the needs of their fellow Christians? The choice was made: visit
the prison. Identify with the incarcerated Christians. It was a
costly decision. Their property was plundered.

This application of what they knew and felt was empowered by
joy. "You *joyfully* accepted the plundering of your property." As
with the case of Jesus in Hebrews 12:2, it was the joy set before
them that enabled them to endure the "cross" of their possessions
being plundered. "You knew that you yourselves had a better
possession and an abiding one." Better and abiding. The joy they
anticipated beyond this life was better than anything this world
could give, and it would never cease. That hope streamed back into
their hearts, and in the midst of suffering, they "*joyfully* accepted
the plundering." They were sustained by the present experience
of the joy of hope. As Paul says in Romans 5:2, "We rejoice in
hope of the glory of God."

God's Aim to Be Visibly Glorified

There is another reason that God intends for joy in him be expressed in applications of active love. The first reason we have seen

is that the very nature of joy in God is expansive. It is a kind of dissatisfied contentment. Like God himself, our joy in God moves out to draw others in. The feeling of joy in God finds practical application in the good deeds of love. The other reason God intends for joy in him to be expressed in applications of active love is his purpose to be glorified openly, visibly.

Our feelings of joy in God, or love for God, are invisible to other people. They are in the heart where only God can see. God delights in what he sees when we delight in him. But his purpose is that he be glorified openly, publicly. He did not create a material universe (including human bodies with hands and feet) simply to conceal his invisible spiritual value. "The heavens declare the glory of God" because they are seen (Ps. 19:1). "His invisible attributes, namely, his eternal power and divine nature, have been clearly perceived ever since the creation of the world, in the things that have been made" (Rom. 1:20). God intends the material world to manifest his glory.

Therefore, he intends Christian joy to be made visible by what Christians *do* outwardly. He intends for all they know and feel to be *applied* in active love. Jesus makes this explicit in Matthew 5. He tells us, "Love your enemies and pray for those who persecute you" (5:44). But he had already shown us that such loving treatment of persecutors is sustained by joy—the same hope of joy that we saw in Hebrews 10:34 and 12:2.

> Blessed are you when others revile you and persecute you and utter all kinds of evil against you falsely on my account. Rejoice and be glad, for your reward is great in heaven, for so they persecuted the prophets who were before you. (Matt. 5:11–12)

The hope of reward in heaven streams back into the present in the form of joy and, because of this joy, we are enabled to love those who persecute us. Then comes the connection with visible good works. Jesus says that such Christians who find joy in the midst of persecution are the salt of the earth and the light of the world (Matt. 5:13–15). But it is not merely their joy that is the light of the world. That joy is invisible; it's in the heart. Rather, it is the overflow of that joy in good works: "Let your light shine before others, so that they may *see your good works* and give glory to your Father who is in heaven" (Matt. 5:13–16). Only when the feeling of joy in the midst of persecution is *applied* in particular deeds of love does it become visible how precious and satisfying God is in the hearts of his people.

In his first letter, Peter makes the same point: "Keep your conduct among the Gentiles honorable, so that when they speak against you as evildoers, they may see your good deeds and glorify God on the day of visitation" (1 Pet. 2:12). Both Jesus and Peter point explicitly to the visibility of the glory of God in the *actions* of Christians. This emphasis on visible good deeds that "adorn the doctrine of God" (Titus 2:10) became a dominant teaching in the New Testament, which is evident from this sampling of texts that call for visible good works:

We are [God's] workmanship, created in Christ Jesus for *good works*, which God prepared beforehand, that we should walk in them. (Eph. 2:10)

See that no one repays anyone evil for evil, but always seek to *do good* to one another and to everyone. (1 Thess. 5:15)

They are to *do good*, to be rich in *good works*, to be generous and ready to share. (1 Tim. 6:18)

[Christ] gave himself for us to redeem us from all lawlessness and to purify for himself a people for his own possession who are zealous for *good works*. (Titus 2:14)

I want you to insist on these things, so that those who have believed in God may be careful to devote themselves to *good works*. (Titus 3:8)

Let our people learn to devote themselves to *good works*, so as to help cases of urgent need, and not be unfruitful. (Titus 3:14)

Let us consider how to stir up one another to love and *good works*. (Heb. 10:24)

Do not neglect to *do good* and to share what you have, for such sacrifices are pleasing to God. (Heb. 13:16)

This is the will of God, that by *doing good* you should put to silence the ignorance of foolish people. (1 Pet. 2:15)

How We Discern What to Do

Lifelong learning includes a growing inclination and wisdom to turn knowledge and feelings into visible deeds that glorify God and do good to others. For those of us who are deeply persuaded that this is the calling of all Christians (2 Thess. 1:1–12), the question becomes, How then shall we discern the path of wisdom?

How shall we recognize, out of the hundreds of possibilities, which good works we should pursue?

Depending on how we ask this question, it might betray a misunderstanding of what we have been doing up to this point in the book. What we have been doing is, in fact, answering that question. Observing, understanding, evaluating, and feeling is our answer to the question, How shall we discern the path of wisdom? How shall we recognize which good works we should pursue? Let's open the lens for a moment and get in focus the wider picture of the four habits of mind and heart that have led to the point of active application in God-glorifying deeds of love.

Discerning Wisdom by Observation

We gain wisdom for application by *observing* the world around us. "Go to the ant, O sluggard; consider her ways, and be *wise*" (Prov. 6:6). Consider and be wise. If we close our eyes and ears to the world around us—the world of nature and the world of man—we will not act wisely. When the blind lead the blind, they fall into a ditch (Matt. 15:14). In the parable of the good Samaritan, which is an *application* of the command to love your neighbor as yourself (Luke 10:27–29), Jesus says of the Samaritan, "A Samaritan, as he journeyed, came to where he was, and when he *saw* [the wounded man], he had compassion" (Luke 10:33). First, there is seeing. Then compassion. Then action. It starts with seeing. If we don't see, we won't love. Seeing is not enough (the priest and Levite saw and passed by on the other side), but it is necessary. We cannot make wise applications of facts we do not have.

Discerning Wisdom by Understanding

We gain wisdom for application by thinking and *understanding*. Observation is not enough. Facts are not enough. One must think. One must put several facts together and draw out a meaning. Was the wounded man in the ditch really wounded, or was he a decoy planted there by a band of robbers? The Samaritan saw enough to persuade him: this man is really wounded and needs my help.

Paul says that as we seek to "make the best use of the time," we should "not be foolish, but *understand* what the will of the Lord is" (Eph. 5:17). Not just see, but understand. The word "understand" in this verse (*syniete*) is the verb form of the noun "understanding" in 2 Timothy 2:7: "Think over what I say, for the Lord will give you *understanding* [*synesin*] in everything." Both observation and thinking are essential. If we think poorly, and draw false inferences from what we observe, our efforts to apply our knowledge with love will probably go awry.

Discerning Wisdom by Evaluation

We gain wisdom for application by evaluating options according to God's worth and God's word. This requires a renewed mind. That's why Paul said in Romans 12:2:

> Do not be conformed to this world, but be transformed by the renewal of your mind, that by testing you may discern what is the will of God, what is good and acceptable and perfect.

This renewal of the mind begins decisively with the change that takes place when the "mind of the flesh" is replaced with the "mind of the Spirit"—that is, when the merely human, fallen mindset, is replaced with a mindset formed and guided by the Holy Spirit. This happens when the Holy Spirit enters a person's life and subdues the hostility to God and replaces it with faith in Christ that treasures God and his ways above other things:

> The mind of the flesh is death, but the mind of the Spirit is life and peace. For the mind of the flesh is hostile to God, for it does not submit to God's law; indeed, it cannot. Those who are in the flesh cannot please God. You, however, are not in the flesh but in the Spirit, if in fact the Spirit of God dwells in you. Anyone who does not have the Spirit of Christ does not belong to him. (Rom. 8:6–9)

This decisive change, which happens at the new birth (John 3:6), leads to an ongoing process and is an essential part of lifelong learning. Thus Paul says, "Put off your old self, which belongs to your former manner of life and is corrupt through deceitful desires, and . . . be renewed in the spirit of your minds" (Eph. 4:22–23). The "spirit of your minds" includes not just the powers of logic, but the ability of the mind to evaluate things truly.

Because of this new spirit of the mind, Paul says, "By testing you may discern [*dokimazein*] what is the will of God, what is good and acceptable and perfect" (Rom. 12:2). This same Greek word for testing—evaluating—is found in Philippians 1:9–10 where Paul prays "that your love may abound more and more, with knowledge and all discernment, so that you may approve [*dokimazein*] what is excellent." He is praying for the ongoing transformation of the Christian mind with "knowledge and all discernment" so that our Christian love will be able to evaluate and discern the excellent way of wise application. When our renewed mind is at its best, we are able to "test [*dokimazete*] everything [and] hold fast what is good" (1 Thess. 5:21).

Discerning Wisdom by Feeling

The birth of new affections for God and his ways enables us both to see and to desire the path of wise application. As long as we are *dis*approving of God and his ways (Rom. 1:28; 8:7), we will suppress the truth (Rom. 1:18). That is, we will not see reality for what it really is. We will see but not see (Matt. 13:13). Our not wanting God and his ways prevents us from seeing them for the treasure that they are. "Deceitful desires" distort the mind's eye (Eph. 4:22).

But when our minds and hearts feel the value of Christ and his ways above all things (Phil. 3:7–8), we are able to see reality for what it is. God ceases to be an ugly or boring or fearful threat to our happiness, and becomes our Father, our Savior, our treasure. And with this new seeing comes a new savoring. A new desire. Therefore, the path of wise application is not only more visible; it is also more desirable. Seeing and savoring according to God's will is a great help in discerning and choosing the actions that glorify God and bless people.

Five Ways of Pursing All the Habits of Mind and Heart

What then is the answer to the question, How shall we recognize, out of the hundreds of possibilities, which good works we should pursue? The first part of the answer is to grow in the habits of heart and mind this book is trying to describe. There is another part to the answer. Built into the preceding chapters are five ways of pursuing the six habits of mind we are commending. Someone might suggest that these five steps are themselves distinct habits of mind and heart in addition to the six we are unfolding. But it seems to me that they are not *in addition to* these six, but rather ways of growing in each of the six. All of them have been pointed out along the way.

1. Meditate on the Word of God

Saturate all six habits of mind and heart with the word of God, the Bible. Nothing is more formative of the renewed mind than the influence of God's word. Read it continually and meditate on it earnestly. The design of the Bible, in revealing God and his ways, is to cause our observing and understanding and evaluating and feeling to overflow in the application of "every good deed"—every good deed that God has appointed for us to do.

> All Scripture is breathed out by God and profitable for teaching, for reproof, for correction, and for training in righteousness, that the man of God may be complete, equipped for *every good work*. (2 Tim. 3:16–17)

The Bible aims to help us know and do the good works that glorify God and love people. It is practical. It bends toward application.

2. Pray for Discernment

Few things are clearer than that God has designed prayer as the way he gives discernment for application. I hope it has been clear that every one of the six habits of mind and heart are to be pursued in prayer. We are always dependent on God for the success of each of these habits. This is especially obvious and urgent when it comes to application.

> It is my prayer that your love may abound more and more, with knowledge and all discernment, so that you may approve what is excellent, and so be pure and blameless for the day of Christ, filled with the fruits of righteousness that come through Jesus Christ to the glory and praise of God. (Phil. 1:9–11)

What is the excellent way? What is the path of purity? Where do the fruits of righteousness come from? How shall my choices bring glory and praise to God? The first answer of this text is that Paul is *praying*! And so should we.

The second answer is that he is praying because a God-glorifying life of purity and excellence is a *gift*. "It is God who works in you, both to will and to work for his good pleasure" (Phil. 2:13). "I will put my Spirit within you, and cause you to walk in my statutes" (Ezek. 36:27). "May the God of peace . . . equip you with everything good that you may do his will, working in us that which is pleasing in his sight" (Heb. 13:20–21). The application of all we know and feel in Christ-exalting love is a gift. A free, undeserved, blood-bought gift of God (Rom. 8:32).

Which does not mean we are passive. What it means is that we act in faith. We act, trusting that in our acting, God freely acts to help us and guide us. The works of love are "works of faith" (1 Thess. 1:3; cf. 2 Thess. 1:11). "The life I now live in the flesh I live by faith in the Son of God" (Gal. 2:20). "Whoever serves, [let him do so] as one who serves by the strength that God supplies—in order that in everything God may be glorified through Jesus Christ" (1 Pet. 4:11). We act by trusting in his action. We say, "Not I but Christ." "I worked harder than any of them, though it was not I, but the grace of God that is with me" (1 Cor. 15:10). All the while we *pray* for the promised help and guidance (Ps. 25:8–10; Heb. 13:5–6).

3. Live in Bible-Saturated Community

God has designed us to pursue the six habits of mind and heart in Christian community. This includes the ministry of dead saints in our lives through their books. But what I have in mind here is the crucial importance of a healthy local church when we are wrestling with how to apply our knowledge in practical choices. The Bible says that Christ has set his people in churches with teachers for the purpose of bringing us to the kind of maturity of those who are not "tossed to and fro by . . . every wind of doctrine" (Eph. 4:12–14). That is, the church is designed to keep us from immature beliefs and actions.

More specifically, the church is designed to equip and motivate us for good works. That is, for application of what we know in God-glorifying and loving ways.

> Let us consider how to stir up one another to *love and good works*, not neglecting to meet together, as is the habit of some, but encouraging one another, and all the more as you see the Day drawing near. (Heb. 10:24–25)

Just when many people will be saying in the last days, "We don't need church," this inspired writer says, you will need church "all the more as you see the Day drawing near." Why? Because it is one of God's essential means of enabling us to apply what we know in the kind of good works that will be crucial in those days.

4. Be Aware of Your God-Given Aptitudes

There are always more good ways to apply what you know than are possible for any one person to do. Nor is it possible to reason out what the most fruitful effects of an action will be for the glory of God and the good of others. God can take the most unlikely application of love and make it fruitful beyond our wildest imagination. And he is able to take an application with great prospects of fruitfulness and render it fruitless. Choices in life almost never come down to accurate calculations of future fruitfulness.

One of the factors that we should take into account when planning a life of wise and helpful application of what we know and feel is our own God-given aptitude. What we mean by "aptitude" is what we are naturally good at and feel at home doing. I don't mean that this is static. You might feel incompetent at a skill in one season of your life, and later discover that you are good at it and love it. Nor do I mean that just because you are good at something you should do it. For one, it may be sinful. For another, you may be good at more than one thing. And for another, God can make you more fruitful in love for his glory by helping you do something you are not very good at. He may want to humble you and glorify himself by using you in your weakness.

Nevertheless, God ordinarily gives us *natural* abilities because he intends to use them. "*Spiritual* gifts" are often *natural* abilities that have been sanctified and empowered by the Holy Spirit. This is where aptitude comes in. We think God's ordinary way of working in his children is for him to sanctify and empower what they are good at by nature and what they feel at home doing.

One of the reasons I think this is the way Paul speaks of "gifts" in Romans 12:6–8:

Having gifts that differ according to the grace given to us, let us use them: if prophecy, in proportion to our faith; if service, in our serving; the one who teaches, in his teaching; the one who exhorts, in his exhortation; the one who contributes, in generosity; the one who leads, with zeal; the one who does acts of mercy, with cheerfulness.

What stands out in this text is that several of these "gifts" are practices that are expected of *all* Christians, not just some gifted Christians. For example, all Christians are expected to "exhort" (Heb. 3:13). All Christians are expected to "contribute" (Eph. 4:28; 1 Tim. 6:18). All Christians are expected to do "acts of mercy" (Luke 10:37). What, then, does it mean to say that these are "gifts that differ according to the grace given to us" (Rom. 12:6)? My answer is that, even though God calls all of us to exhort, contribute, and show mercy, nevertheless some people have a special aptitude for this. It seems to be as natural for them as being right-handed or being able to carry a tune. God purifies and empowers and blesses that aptitude in special ways.

So in our quest for lifelong learning, we should not ignore our God-given aptitudes. We should know them and seek to dedicate them utterly to the glory of Christ. Whatever our vocation, and whatever our hobbies and whatever ways we serve our church and communities, we should seek to consecrate it all to Christ. In this way, our aptitudes become a path toward wise and fruitful application of what we know and feel. Our aptitudes turn out to be God's way of magnifying his worth and doing good to others.

5. Acknowledge with Thankfulness God's Providence

Finally, the pervasive, all-inclusive sovereignty of God (Isa. 46:10; Eph. 1:11; James 4:15) means that you are where you are by his design. It may be prison. It may be the governor's mansion. This means that millions of good deeds are out of your reach. They are in another town and another country. This means that your time and location with all their limitations are God-appointed.

This does not mean you are forbidden to change your location—across the hall or across the world. But it does mean that at this moment—at any moment—you are where you are. And you are there by God's design. This is true of nations and individuals. "[God] made from one man every nation of mankind to live on all the face of the earth, *having determined allotted periods and the boundaries of their dwelling place*" (Acts 17:26).

The effect of this realization should be that we not spend all our energies trying to make our situation different. If it is painful or sinful, by all means, do what you can to change the situation. But trust the providence of God. That is, trust his purposeful sovereignty.[1] You are where you are for a reason. You may not be there tomorrow.

---

1 To dig more deeply into the doctrine of God's providence, see John Piper, *Providence* (Wheaton, IL: Crossway, 2022).

This really does become an adventure when you think about it. You will never have just this place and this moment again. It is, therefore, a unique appointment from God. Ten thousand good deeds are not possible in this place and this moment. But several are. A word. A gesture. An act. God's providence is your appointment. All that you have observed and understood and evaluated and felt, in God's providence, has brought you to this moment and place. Embrace God's wisdom in this. Open your eyes. Act here and now for the glory of God and the good of others.

Habits of Heart and Mind Coming to Fruition

Lifelong learning is meant to lead to the active application of what we know for the good of others and the glory of God. Observing and understanding and evaluating are for the sake of joy in God that overflows in a thousand applications of doing good. And since it is more blessed to give than to receive (Acts 20:35), these active good deeds make our joy in God even greater, as it seeks to expand by including others in it.

The vocational and nonvocational variety of these good deeds is immeasurable. But we should not be paralyzed by endless possibilities of application. In the formation of the six habits of mind and heart, God is fitting us for wise action. And when the pursuit of these habits is saturated with God's word and prayer in a healthy church, we may be confident that the purpose of God's providence for our place and aptitude will come to fruition in wise action that honors him and blesses others.

6

Expression

*We want to grow for a lifetime in our ability to
express in speech and writing what we have observed,
understood, evaluated, felt, and applied.*

BY *EXPRESSION*, I MEAN PRIMARILY the verbal communication
of what we have observed, understood, evaluated, and felt through
written or spoken (or signed) language. The expression through
deeds was the main focus of the previous chapter on application. So
you can see that *expression* is, in fact, a subcategory of *application*.
We can apply what we know by *doing*, and we can apply what we
know by *speaking* or *writing*, which is a kind of doing. So we might
have limited ourselves to five habits of mind and heart instead of
six. We might have treated *expression* as part of *application*. But it
seems to me that the practice of communication by speaking and
writing is so vital to a fruitful life, and therefore so prominent in
the educational process, it should receive its own focus.

The reason I speak of *expression* as a "*habit* of heart and mind" is that there is a way our words should be habitually used. Most broadly, I want to encourage you to grow in using words for the glory of God and the good of people. When Paul said, "Whatever you do, in *word* or deed, do everything in the name of the Lord Jesus" (Col. 3:17), what did he mean, that every word should be spoken "in the name of the Lord Jesus"? I think he meant that all of our words should be spoken in reliance on the Lord Jesus, and conformed to the truth and ways of the Lord Jesus, and spoken ultimately for the glory of the Lord Jesus. This will not only glorify God in Christ, but will also be good for people, so that Paul's other command will happen at the same time: "Let all that you do [in word and deed] be done in love" (1 Cor. 16:14).

God Himself Has Spoken

Like the air we breathe, language is so much a part of our lives that we can easily miss how utterly crucial it is for existence—natural existence and eternal existence. All natural existence was created and is sustained by the *word* of God. "By faith we understand that the universe was created by the *word* of God" (Heb. 11:3). And "he upholds the universe by the *word* of his power" (Heb. 1:3). And all eternal existence—the gift of eternal life in Christ was created in us by the word of God: "Of his own will he brought us forth by the *word* of truth, that we should be a kind of firstfruits of his creatures" (James 1:18). Indeed, all language started with God. Even before creation, the second person of the Trinity is called "the Word" (John 1:1).

Therefore, all of creation is a kind of language—spoken by God and revealing God. But more clearly and decisively, God revealed himself through human language in the Bible. In the

Old Testament, 290 times we read the phrase, "Thus says the Lord"; 267 times in the Old Testament, we read, ". . . declares the Lord." "All *Scripture* [the writings] is breathed out by God" (2 Tim. 3:16). "Men *spoke* from God as they were carried along by the Holy Spirit" (2 Pet. 1:21).

Not only has God spoken and revealed himself in human language, but he made *us* to be speakers like him. Animals communicate in their rudimentary ways. But the richness of human language—carrying mental reflections and heart affections—is a unique gift of God to humans, primarily for communicating with God and with each other about God—including speaking about all the world which is God's (1 Cor. 10:26). He has ordained that salvation come to us through words: "Faith comes from *hearing*, and hearing through the *word* of Christ" (Rom. 10:17). "It pleased God through the folly of what we *preach* to save those who believe" (1 Cor. 1:21).

How Much Do Our Words Matter?

There is great power in the use of language. Enough to make us tremble in the use of our words. "Death and life are in the power of the tongue" (Prov. 18:21). "The mouth of the righteous is a fountain of life" (Prov. 10:11). "A gentle tongue is a tree of life, but perverseness in it breaks the spirit" (Prov. 15:4). For good and evil, the tongue is powerful. It has potential for imparting grace (Eph. 4:29) or spreading misery like a "scorching fire" (Prov. 16:27).

Of all the wisdom that abounds in the biblical book of James, nothing gets more space than the tongue. James portrays our capacity for language as so unruly that it is the hardest part of our lives to get under control.

If anyone does not stumble in what he *says*, he is a perfect man, able also to bridle his whole body. If we put bits into the mouths of horses so that they obey us, we guide their whole bodies as well. Look at the ships also: though they are so large and are driven by strong winds, they are guided by a very small rudder wherever the will of the pilot directs. So also the tongue is a small member, yet it boasts of great things. How great a forest is set ablaze by such a small fire! And the tongue is a fire, a world of unrighteousness. The tongue is set among our members, staining the whole body, setting on fire the entire course of life, and set on fire by hell. For every kind of beast and bird, of reptile and sea creature, can be tamed and has been tamed by mankind, but no human being can tame the tongue. It is a restless evil, full of deadly poison. With it we bless our Lord and Father, and with it we curse people who are made in the likeness of God. From the same mouth come blessing and cursing. My brothers, these things ought not to be so. (James 3:1–10)

Therefore, it is clear that how we use our tongue—how we speak—really matters. That is an understatement. To underline the seriousness of what is at stake in the way we speak, Jesus reminds us that the mouth is the bellwether of the heart. And on the last day our words will be brought forth as evidence of the genuineness of our Christianity.

The good person out of his good treasure brings forth good, and the evil person out of his evil treasure brings forth evil. I tell you, on the day of judgment people will give account for every careless word they speak, for by your words you will be justified, and by your words you will be condemned. (Matt. 12:35–37)

So if we desire to grow in this habit of expressing ourselves in Christ-exalting, grace-imparting ways, what traits should mark our speech and writing? I suppose one might say that they should be marked by every virtue that characterizes a mature Christian in general. In a sense, then, everything that the Bible teaches about how to be a God-glorifying, people-loving person applies to our words. But there are seven traits of Christian speaking and writing I want to call out for special focus.

1. Our Words Should Be True

"God . . . never lies" (Titus 1:2). He is the "God of truth" (Isa. 65:16). His Spirit is the "Spirit of truth" (John 14:17). And his Son *is* the truth (John 14:6). Paul protests against every possible indictment of God: "Let God be true though every one were a liar" (Rom. 3:4). So we could base our commitment to truthfulness on the imitation of God. "Be imitators of God, as beloved children" (Eph. 5:1). He never lies. We should never lie.

But the commitment to truth is rooted more deeply than in imitation. God is not simply the infinitely reliable nonliar. He is the ground of truth itself. He is the source of all truth. He is therefore the measure of all truth. So, we don't just imitate his truth-telling; we measure all our assertions by his nature—his worth, his character, his attributes. The truth of our words means that what we are trying to communicate corresponds to reality. And God is the ultimate reality that defines the true nature of all other reality.

When we do not tell the truth, we betray God, not only by failing to act the way he acts, and not only by failing to conform our meaning to his reality, but also by failing to trust his promises. What motive would there be to lie if we really believed that God cares for us (1 Pet. 5:7), and is pursuing our good with omnipotent affection (Jer. 32:41), and has forgiven all our sins (Rom. 4:7), and will give us everything we need (Rom. 8:32; Phil. 4:19), so that we do not need to fear anyone (Heb. 13:5–6)? We do not need to curry anyone's favor or sully anyone's reputation. We do not need to tell people they are better than they are (flattery, Prov. 26:28), nor make people look worse than they are (slander, 1 Pet. 2:1). God has our back. We can tell the truth and trust him.

The whole being of a Christian should be truthful through and through. We are children of light, not darkness (Eph. 5:8). We have been saved by "the word of truth, the gospel" (Eph. 1:13). Which means that there are profound foundations beneath the biblical demands for truthfulness. They don't float rootless in the air. "You shall not bear false witness" (Ex. 20:16). "You shall not lie to one another" (Lev. 19:11). "Having put away falsehood, let each one of you speak the truth with his neighbor" (Eph. 4:25). "Do not lie to one another, seeing that you have put off the old self with its practices" (Col. 3:9). Trying to make our lives easier by distorting the truth is not part of who we are anymore. Lying has died with the "old self." The Christian habit of expression is the habit of truth.

2. Our Words Should Be Clear

If we love the truth, we will love clarity in speaking the truth, because the value of truth for others is in its being communicated clearly. Christians love people. Therefore, we do not want to keep them in the dark but bring them into the light of truth. Being unclear is a mark of incompetence or insecurity or deviousness. We may simply be unable to state things clearly. Or we may shy away from being too plain for fear that the truth may offend. Or we may intentionally desire to deceive. Being unclear may be innocent or sinful. But in either case it is not exemplary, and our aim in lifelong learning is to grow in our ability to speak and write so that the truth we are trying to communicate is crystal clear.

Defining Terms

This means we will define our terms if there is serious doubt that our listeners don't know what we mean by particular words or concepts. In chapter 2, we spoke of "coming to terms" when we read what others have written. That means making sure that the meaning of a word is the same in the writer's mind and the reader's mind. We will not be clear if we use the word *rock*, meaning a large stone, but another person thinks we mean *rock* as a kind of music. We are being unclear. We are assuming too much.

Coming to terms means making sure that does not happen. And it is mainly the speaker's or writer's responsibility. Many arguments would simply not happen if discussions put a priority on everyone knowing what everyone else means by their words and concepts. A person who does not care about defining terms probably is motivated not by a loving desire to communicate but by a desire to hear himself talk, or make a power move.

Clarity through Order

Clarity depends not only on coming to terms but also on orderly thought. It is possible to say many true things, but to say them in such a jumble that no one can follow our meaning. When Luke decided to write his two-volume work of Luke-Acts in the New Testament, he said this about his goal: "It seemed good to me also, having followed all things closely for some time past, to write *an orderly account* for you, most excellent Theophilus, that you may have certainty concerning the things you have been taught" (Luke 1:3–4). The word for "orderly account" pertains to "being in sequence in time, space, or logic."[1]

The aim of this orderliness is clarity. We don't want people to get lost in what we are trying to say. If we care about the reader (or the listener), we will care about putting our thoughts together in a way that helps them follow what we think. Of course, it is a truism that the failure to be clear for others is often owing to the fact that we are not clear to ourselves. We are not sure what we think. Obviously then there is some work that needs to be done in our own thinking if we are to speak clearly.

Intentional Ambiguity?

Someone might want to remind us that there is an exception to what we are saying, namely, intentional ambiguity. Jesus used intentional ambiguity in some of his parables. For example, when his disciples asked why he was speaking in parables, he said:

---

1 W. Bauer, F. W. Danker, W. Arndt, and F. W. Gingrich, *A Greek-English Lexicon of the New Testament and Other Early Christian Literature*, 3rd ed. (Chicago: University of Chicago Press, 1999), 490.

To you has been given the secret of the kingdom of God, but for those outside everything is in parables, so that "they may indeed see but not perceive, and may indeed hear but not understand, lest they should turn and be forgiven." (Mark 4:11–12)

In other words, Jesus was consigning those who would not be his disciples to a kind of judicial ignorance. It was a kind of judgment. He was handing them over to their sinfulness. We are not denying that there may be rare occasions when a Christian will have wise reasons for intentional ambiguity. For example, if a four-year-old asks about sexual intercourse or the meaning of daddy's heart surgery, a wise parent will say something vague, not to mislead the child, but to postpone full clarity until he is capable of understanding.

There is a more positive use of intentional ambiguity. When writing poetry, for example, we may choose language that has a double meaning, or we may make a point indirectly rather than directly. Two things should be said about the fact that poetry is often less clear than language that aims at precision and accuracy. First, the very form of poetry alerts the reader to adjust his expectations and to read the poem the way the author intends, by enjoying the way the author comes at things with images, for example, rather than definitions. Second, even the indirectness of poetry can serve the truth if the poet believes in truth and wants to communicate something true.

Nevertheless, granting some exceptions, the pervasive commitment of the Christian will be to clarity. The apostle Paul put a huge premium on this: "We have renounced disgraceful, underhanded ways. We refuse to practice cunning or to tamper with God's word, but by the open statement of the truth we would commend ourselves to everyone's conscience in the sight of God" (2 Cor. 4:2). "Open statement of the truth" means not just "speak truth," but speak it with as much openness and clarity as one can.

Clarity and Edification

One of his chief motives in this kind of commitment to clarity is that without it, people will not be "built up" in their faith. Paul insisted that in the Christian gatherings at Corinth, people not speak in ways that others could not understand. "If you give thanks with your spirit, how can anyone in the position of an outsider say 'Amen' to your thanksgiving when *he does not know what you are saying*? For you may be giving thanks well enough, but the other person is *not being built up*" (1 Cor. 14:16–17). To emphasize the point, he says, "In church I would rather speak five words with my mind in order to instruct others, than ten thousand words in a tongue" (1 Cor. 14:19). If we love people—if we hope that our words will build them up—we will join Paul in his commitment to clarity.

3. Our Words Should Be Authentic

The Christian communicator values authenticity, honesty, sincerity. The difference between being authentic and being truthful is that being truthful means that what we say corresponds to the facts, while being authentic means that what we say corresponds to our heart. The opposite of authenticity is hypocrisy. This means that our words are artificial; they don't represent an honest portrayal of what is going on in our deeper selves.

The apostle Paul again sets the pattern for us with this profound example of authenticity: "We are not, like so many, peddlers of God's word, but as men of *sincerity* as from God, in the sight of God we speak in Christ" (2 Cor. 2:17). This is an amazing statement. There is a negative statement and a positive one.

Negative: We don't peddle God's word. In other words, our speaking is not motivated by a desire for money. That would be utterly inauthentic—to say all kinds of true things about the way God saves sinners, only to be motivated by the love of money. That is the essence of inauthenticity.

Positive: We speak God's word in four ways. (1) "Sincerely,"[2] honestly and authentically motivated in our hearts by the reality we speak with our mouths. (2) "As from God, not speaking our own word on our own authority. We are utterly dependent for content and for authority on God. (3) "In the sight of God," giving an account to him above any human person, responsible to him, assessed by him. (4) "In Christ," resting for our acceptance with God on our union with Christ and empowered by that union to act with authentic motives of love, as he is love.

Appropriate Emotion

We include in this call to authenticity the call to appropriate emotion. This is not the same as authenticity, because if you don't feel an appropriate emotion, you still may be authentic by avoiding

2 Greek *eilikrineias*, meaning "the quality or state of being free of dissimulation, *sincerity, purity of motive.*" Bauer, Danker, Arndt, and Gingrich, *Greek-English Lexicon*, 282.

fake efforts to show the emotion, or by simply admitting to your listeners that you don't feel what you should. But we hope that when we lack fitting emotions, our response would the authentic pursuit of those emotions we lack.

Authentic expression of no emotion or a wrong emotion or a disproportionate emotion is better than deception. But far better is the pursuit of true and proportionate emotion. Speaking at a funeral and speaking at a wedding call for different kinds of emotion. The goal of authenticity is not the ability to honestly tell the wedding guests you feel no joy. The goal is to feel what you ought to feel, and share it with authenticity.[3]

One of the marks of authenticity of speech is the readiness to say what you mean and stop, allowing for silence or for others to speak. In other words, you don't feel driven to keep talking for fear that silence or other viewpoints might expose your error. This is one reason the proverb says, "When words are many, transgression is not lacking" (Prov. 10:19). Words are meant to reveal the heart honestly. But inauthentic words do the opposite. They conceal unworthy intentions, and to do that successfully they often go on and on. "Therefore, let your words be few. For a dream comes with much business, and a fool's voice with many words" (Eccl. 5:2–3).

Authentic speech may be risky. It is a form of humble and wise transparency. Not everything in the heart must come out in every setting. Wisdom and love may motivate both speech and silence. But there is a world of difference between that kind of loving restraint and the inauthentic use of words to conceal one's

3 For my thought on how to pursue proper feelings that you don't feel, see pp. 106–14.

true feelings. Over a lifetime of learning, my hope is that we all would be growing in the habit of humble and wise authenticity in the expression of what we know and feel.

4. Our Words Should Be Thoughtful

I admit to some difficulty in finding the right word for what I have in mind here. By "thoughtful," I don't mean considerate or caring. To be sure, considerateness and care are the goals of all these traits of expression. They are part of what I mean by love for others, and that is the goal of all application and expression.

What I mean is the opposite of *glib* or *trivial* or *empty*. What positive word would you choose as the opposite of those traits? I thought I could use *serious*, but most people think of *serious* in a much too narrow way, like *grim* or *somber*, which is not what I mean. I thought I could use *substantial*, but most people would probably think of *sizeable*, which is not what I mean. Perhaps *significant* comes closest. Maybe you can come up with a better word.

What I want to say is that Christians should not be like those Paul refers to in Titus 1:10: "There are many who are insubordinate, *empty talkers*." Believe it or not, the standard scholarly lexicon defines this word for "empty talker" (*mataiologos*) as "windbag."[4] Our concern here is with people who seem incapable of seriousness. They feel awkward around people who are discussing something weighty (substantial, serious, significant). Their default is to say something clever or make a pun or redirect the conversation onto something lighthearted. This is not a healthy sign. Life is too precious and short for the normal disposition to be cavalier or trivial or frivolous.

4 Bauer, Danker, Arndt, and Gingrich, *Greek-English Lexicon*, 621.

Humor

I do not mean by "substantial" and "serious" and "significant" that there is no place for humor. But there is a difference between a spontaneous, robust belly laugh at the surprising foibles of life and the often cynical chortle at everything. Charles Spurgeon gets it exactly right:

> We must conquer—some of us especially—our tendency to levity. A great distinction exists between holy cheerfulness, which is a virtue, and that general levity, which is a vice. There is a levity which has not enough heart to laugh, but trifles with everything; it is flippant, hollow, unreal. A hearty laugh is no more levity and a heart cry.[5]

Unbroken seriousness of a melodramatic or somber kind will inevitably communicate a sickness of soul to most people. This is partly because life as God created it is not like that. There are, for example, little babies in the world who are not the least impressed with our excessive earnestness. They are cooing and smiling and calling for their daddies to get down on the floor and play with them. The daddy who cannot do this with delight will not understand the true seriousness of sin, because he is not capable of enjoying what God has preserved from its ravages. He is really a sick man and unfit to lead others to health. Earnestness is good. Very good. But he is in the end earnest about being earnest, not earnest about being joyful. The real battle in life is to be as happy in God as we

5 Charles Spurgeon, *Lectures to My Students* (Grand Rapids, MI: Zondervan, 1972), 212.

can be, and that takes a very special kind of earnestness, since God threatens terrible things if we will not be happy (Deut. 28:47).

The habit of *thoughtful* expression is a steadying influence. It creates the sense in others that the thoughtful speaker will not embarrass anyone by levity when seriousness is needed, by trifling when something significant is needed, or by foolishness when something wise is needed. People around the *thoughtful* person have confidence that he is thinking wisely about the spirit of the moment and will have something significant to say when needed.

5. Our Words Should Be Creative

I don't mean that everyone is called to be a poet or a writer of imaginative literature. What I mean is that we should aspire to grow over a lifetime in our ability to select words and arrange words and deliver words in fresh ways that have the greatest impact for good on others. The aim is not that we all write poems but that we all try to use language in ways that attract people to pay attention to what we have to say, and overtime expect to hear us with pleasure and profit.

Being interesting about the best news in the world is a virtue. Christians know the best news. It is endlessly interesting. There are heights and depths and lengths and breadths (Eph. 3:18) that are inexhaustible. The gospel is not boring. To communicate it as though it were boring is a sin. One way we should seek to awaken attention and interest is by the creativity of our language. What words do we choose? How shall we put them together? How shall we deliver them—orally or in writing? These are questions of creativity and hoped-for impact.

Thief in the Night

An example of creative use of words would be Jesus's shocking comparison of the coming of the Son of Man with the coming of a thief at night:

> Know this, that if the master of the house had known at what hour the thief was coming, he would not have left his house to be broken into. You also must be ready, for the Son of Man is coming at an hour you do not expect. (Luke 12:39–40)

One can imagine the disciples glancing at each other: Did he just say what I think he said? The glorious coming of the Son of Man at the end of the age, compared to a thief! This is creative in the sense that it is out of the ordinary. The mind creatively casts about beyond the ordinary use of words and hits upon some words that will provoke and interest and hold attention and force one to think over what he just said.

Concrete, Not Abstract

Another mark of the creative use of words is concreteness—speaking with specific examples that one can see or taste or touch or hear or smell. This is the opposite of generalizations or abstractions. Our attention and interest are awakened and held more by specifics than by generalities, and more by concrete examples than by abstractions. So, for example, peach rather than fruit; dog rather than animal; rain rather than weather; Neptune rather than planet; basketball rather than sport; buttered toast and bacon rather than breakfast; brown woolen pullover rather than clothing; rusty socket wrench rather than tool. Jon and David rather than friends.

Mark Twain once said, "The difference between the almost right word and the right word is . . . the difference between the lightning bug and the lightning."[6] And in saying it just like that, he illustrated the very thing he was talking about. The contrast between lightning bug and lightning gets our attention, makes us smile at the concreteness and vastness of the difference, and inspires us to do the same.

Don't get me wrong. Abstraction—generalization—is good and often absolutely necessary for life. If you only know how the traffic rules apply to this solitary, concrete, nonabstract, very real stoplight on this specific corner, and no others, you shouldn't drive. We survive by abstracting principles from specifics and turning them in to generalizations without which we cannot live. People don't want to come away from your communication with truth that applies only to the maple tree in your front yard. But referring to that very specific tree may clarify the principle perfectly.

God has given us five senses. We smell the honeysuckle. We see the Dogwood blossoms. We hear the cooing of the dove. We taste the spicy Chick-fil-A sandwich. And we feel the biting ten-below windchill on our face. To be sure, we are rational, abstracting beings. But God made us more immediately sentient beings. Creative links with this part of our nature through words is a worthy goal of lifelong learning.

When Paul says, "Let your speech always be gracious, seasoned with salt" (Col. 4:6), he meant that our speech should not be bland and tasteless. Rather, just like salt makes food more enjoyable, so we should seek to make our words effective. Salty speech would

6 Cited in "Respectfully Quoted: A Dictionary of Quotations," Bartleby, accessed May 11, 2014, http://www.bartleby.com/.

sound something like this: "A word fitly spoken is like apples of gold in a setting of silver" (Prov. 25:11). Our words should seek to be pleasing to the ear as "apples of gold in a setting of silver" is pleasing to the eye.

The Bible is filled with every kind of literary device to increase the impact of its language: acrostic, alliteration, analogy, anthropomorphism, assonance, cadence, chiasm, consonance, dialogue, hyperbole, irony, metaphor, meter, onomatopoeia, paradox, parallelism, repetition, rhyme, satire, simile—they're all there, and more. If we are Bible saturated, our language will naturally share in this kind of creativity.

Danger of Eloquence

At this point, we meet a problem. Does the apostle Paul actually tell us not to be creative in this way as we try to communicate the truth of Christ? He says in 1 Corinthians 1:17, "Christ did not send me to baptize but to preach the gospel, and *not with words of eloquent wisdom*, lest the cross of Christ be emptied of its power." And in 1 Corinthians 2:1 he says, "I, when I came to you, brothers, did not come proclaiming to you the testimony of God *with lofty speech or wisdom*." Do these warnings against eloquent wisdom or lofty speech mean we should not make creative efforts to communicate in impactful ways? Does the effort to find human language that is impactful empty the cross of Christ of its power?

My conclusion is that what Paul finds fault with at Corinth is not so much any particular language conventions but the exploitation of language to exalt self and belittle the crucified Lord. The reason "the cross is folly" (1 Cor. 1:18) to the eloquent in Corinth is that the cross is so destructive of human pride. Those who aim at human praise through eloquence can only see the cross as foolishness. The cross is the place our sin is seen as most horrible and God's free grace shines most brightly. Both of these mean we deserve nothing. Therefore, the cross undercuts pride and exalts Christ, not us, and that made it foolish to the eloquent in Corinth.

Therefore, since the Bible is replete with a kind of "eloquence" that creatively uses language for greater impact, and since Paul himself could write with beautiful language, as for example in the great love chapter of 1 Corinthians 13, I conclude that the eloquence he was criticizing, and that we should avoid, had two deadly features. It aimed at self-exaltation, and it did not aim at the exaltation of Christ crucified. Paul's aim—God's aim—was "that no human being might boast in the presence of God" (1 Cor. 1:29), but rather, "Let the one who boasts, boast in the Lord" (1 Cor. 1:31). That is the test we should make of our choice of words and how we use them: do they humble us and exalt Christ?

James Denney (1856–1917) once said, "No man can give the impression that he himself is clever and that Christ is mighty to save."[7] This is a haunting sentence. It is a very pointed warning. It should fly like a banner over our conversations and writing and teaching and preaching.

But does it mean that any conscious effort at creativity necessarily elevates self and obscures the truth that Christ is mighty to save? I don't think so. To be sure, creativity in speech is not the decisive factor in salvation or sanctification; God is. But faith comes by hearing, and hearing by the word. That word

7 Cited in John Stott, *Between Two Worlds: The Art of Preaching in the Twentieth Century* (Grand Rapids, MI: Eerdmans, 1982), 325.

in the Bible is pervasively creative—words are chosen and put together in a way to give great impact. And God invites us to craft our own creative phrases for his name's sake, not ours. And in the mystery of his sovereign grace, he will glorify himself in the hearts of others in spite of, and because of, the words we have chosen. In that way, he will keep us humble and get glory for himself.

6. Our Words Should Be Well-Timed

I have known people with remarkably good ideas and creative words to speak them, but with a poor sense of timing. They say wise things at the wrong time. They seem to lack a sense of the mood of the moment. The book of Proverbs gives both negative and positive examples to urge us on toward wise and helpful timing. "Whoever sings songs to a heavy heart is like one who takes off a garment on a cold day, and like vinegar on soda" (Prov. 25:20). There's nothing wrong with a cheerful song. But not in the hospital room where the spouse just had a heart attack. "To make an apt answer is a joy to a man, and a word in season, how good it is!" (Prov. 15:23).

It is crucial that we discern not only what to say, but when to say it. When our spiritual sensors are working, we discern the need of the moment. That is what Paul seems to be getting at when he says that the only thing that should come out of our mouths is what "is good for building up, as fits the occasion, that it may give grace to those who hear" (Eph. 4:29). "As fits the occasion" refers to the peculiar need of the moment. The wisdom of what to say is determined to a great degree by what we hear. Hearing with wisdom will lead to speaking with wisdom. What comes out of our mouths should be formed by what goes into our ears. Inattentive listeners make tactless speakers.

Have you ever wondered why the book of Job devotes 29 chapters (3–31) mainly to the words of Job's three friends who in the end receive God's rebuke for what they have said (Job 42:7)? It is probably because, while most of their words were in themselves true, they were poorly timed and poorly applied. But what a gift it is when the timing is wise. "The tongue of the wise brings healing" (Prov. 12:18). "The mouth of the righteous is a fountain of life" (Prov. 10:11). "Gracious words are like a honeycomb, sweetness to the soul and health to the body" (Prov. 16:24). But those precious effects of wise words are lost where they are ill-timed. May the Lord make us discerning not only about what to say, but also when to say it.

7. Our Words Should Be Clean

When we consider how the apostle Paul addressed obscenities and filthy language, it is remarkable that he focuses not on the nature of the words themselves but rather on the nature of the motives behind them. Consider these three exhortations:

Let there be no *filthiness nor foolish talk nor crude joking*, which are out of place, but instead let there be thanksgiving. (Eph. 5:4)

Let no *corrupting talk* come out of your mouths, but only such as is good for building up, as fits the occasion, that it may give grace to those who hear. (Eph. 4:29)

You must put them all away: anger, wrath, malice, slander, and *obscene talk* from your mouth . . . seeing that you have

> put off the old self with its practices and have put on the new
> self, which is being renewed in knowledge after the image of
> its creator. (Col. 3:8)

How does Paul make his case for clean language? He contrasts dirty language with thanksgiving, upbuilding grace, and renewal in the image of God.

The heart that defaults to "filthiness," "foolish talk," and "crude joking" is not sufficiently thankful (Eph. 5:4). That is an amazing diagnosis of the problem. But think about it. Does that not prove true in our own experience? The hearts of foul-mouthed people are not brimming with thankfulness. They are generally cynical and angry and resentful that things are not going their way. That is the opposite of the humble posture of amazement that God is so good to undeserving people.

The heart that defaults to "corrupting talk" is not eagerly aiming to build up other people and give them grace. Foul language does not minister grace to anyone (Eph. 4:29). In fact, it tends to infect others with the same angry selfishness that refuses to put a guard at the door of the mouth (Ps. 41:3). The person who uses dirty language is asserting his presumed freedom with little aim to edify or strengthen in grace.

The heart that defaults to "obscene talk" is falling back into the ways of the "old self" and failing to realize that the new self is "being renewed after the image of its creator" (Col. 3:8). People who resort to obscenities are not on a quest to be conformed to Christ. They are not pressing forward in the pursuit of the newness that Christ gives.

So, as we seek to grow in the effectiveness of the expression of what we know and feel, let us aim at thankfulness, and graciousness, and the newness that Christ purchased at the cost of his own blood. These, Paul says, will simply preempt corrupting talk and fill our mouths with what is good for people and an honor to God.

Fruitful Tongue as a Gift of God

We want to grow in our ability to express in speech and writing what we have observed, understood, evaluated, felt, and applied. It is clear that progress in this growth will depend on God's help. Just beneath the surface of everything I have said in this chapter is the truth that what comes out of the mouth is owing to the condition of the heart. "What comes out of the mouth proceeds from the heart" (Matt. 15:18). "Out of the abundance of the heart the mouth speaks" (Matt. 12:34). Therefore, we are dependent on God's heart-transforming work.

He has promised to do it. "I will give you a new heart, and a new spirit I will put within you. And I will remove the heart of stone from your flesh and give you a heart of flesh" (Ezek. 36:26). These are the promises of the new covenant that Christ secured by shedding his own blood (Luke 22:20). "I will put my laws into their minds, and write them on their hearts, and I will be their God, and they shall be my people" (Heb. 8:10). In other words, when God calls us to express ourselves in certain ways, he does not leave us to ourselves. The fruitful tongue is a gift of God.

The Lord GOD has given me
    the tongue of those who are taught,

that I may know how to sustain with a word
    him who is weary. (Isa. 50:4)

Therefore, we do not speak in vain when we pray with the psalmist:

Let the words of my mouth and the meditation of my heart
    be acceptable in your sight,
    O LORD, my rock and my redeemer. (Ps. 19:14)

Conclusion

Foundations for Lifelong Living

OUR AIM IN EDUCATION is to cultivate habits of mind and heart that provide foundations for lifelong learning. Therefore, what we do in the classroom at Bethlehem College and Seminary is relevant for all of life. What we do for an eighteen-year-old is relevant for eighty-somethings. We are never done with this education in serious joy.

We believe that the biblical prayers and commands to *grow* in knowledge and wisdom never cease to apply at any age. "We have not ceased to pray for you asking that you . . . walk worthy of the Lord . . . *increasing* in the knowledge of God" (Col. 1:10). "*Grow* in the grace and knowledge of our Lord and Savior Jesus Christ" (2 Pet. 3:18). "*Get wisdom*, and whatever you get, *get insight*" (Prov. 4:7).

This lifelong growth happens as the six habits of heart and mind are alive and active with the word of God shaping them all. *Observe* accurately, *understand* clearly, *evaluate* fairly, *feel* properly, *apply* wisely, *express* compellingly. When these habits are exercised, the effect is a kind of maturity that makes a person more fruitful in whatever vocation God assigns.

"Men with Chests"

Alan Jacobs expressed this conviction when he described C. S. Lewis's vision of education:

> Lewis passionately believed that education is not about providing information so much as cultivating "habits of the heart"—producing "men with chests," as he puts it in his book *The Abolition of Man*, that is, people who not only *think* as they should but *respond* as they should, instinctively and emotionally, to the challenges and blessings the world offers to them.[1]

The hinge between *observing* and *understanding*, on the one side, and *applying* and *expressing*, on the other side, is *evaluating* and *feeling* in between. Without observing and understanding, there would be no objective basis for evaluation and feeling. Without applying and expressing, all our evaluation and feeling would be egocentric and loveless. "Men with chests" (people who believe in objective evaluation and respond with appropriate feeling) are like trees that have roots in observation and understanding, and branches in application and expression. As Christians, their roots are in God-revealing reality, and their branches are Christ-exalting love.

One way to set the habits of the heart and mind in a biblical framework is to look at Philippians 1:9: "It is my prayer that your *love* may abound more and more, with *knowledge* and all *discernment*." The *aim* is love, and the *means* is knowledge and discernment. What we have tried to show is that the habits of

---

1 Alan Jacobs, *The Narnian: The Life and Imagination of C. S. Lewis* (New York: Harper Collins, 2005), xxiii–iv.

application and *expression* correspond to love for people. And the habits of *observation* and *understanding* correspond to knowledge and discernment. The link between the two is God's supernatural answer to prayer in a transformed heart (chest!) that evaluates and feels with the life of Christ's Spirit.

Lifelong Living

This means that, in a sense, these six foundations in lifelong learning are a way of describing the Christian life. Lifelong learning, in a Christian worldview, is lifelong living—biblical living. True education is not an add-on to faithful Christian living. It is what we do, because of who God is and what he made us to be.

> We *observe* because that's why God gave us physical and spiritual senses.
> We *understand* because that's why God gave us minds.
> We *evaluate* because God revealed himself as the measure of all true worth.
> We *feel* because that's why God gave us hearts and emotions.
> We *apply* and *express* because God calls us to love.

These are the habits of life, not just the habits of education. These are foundations of living, not just foundations of learning. We practice these habits in reliance on God's grace, guided by God's word, for the sake of God's glory. "For from him and through him and to him are all things. To him be glory forever. Amen" (Rom. 11:36).

Appendix

Agassiz and the Fish

AT THE BEGINNING OF my theological studies in my early twenties, an unforgettable inspiration in my growing desire to see, as I had never seen before, was the story of Agassiz and the fish. As I read this story for the first time, I was riveted. It was like a bright explosion on the horizon of my new life of Bible study. The brightness made all the details of the Bible light up. Suddenly I was seeing patterns and interrelationships and lines of thought that I had never seen before. And all of this was happening not because a teacher was telling me what to see, but because someone was telling me, *Look, look, look.*

Louis Agassiz (1807–1873) was the founder of the Harvard Museum of Comparative Zoology and a Harvard professor. One of his students, Samuel Scudder, wrote about how this amazing professor showed him what he could see if only he would form the habit and patience of looking long and hard at the object of his study. His story follows.[1]

1 Horace E. Scudder, ed., *American Poems: Longfellow, Whittier, Bryant, Holmes, Lowell, Emerson; with Biographical Sketches and Notes*, 3rd ed. (Boston: Houghton, Osgood, 1879), 450–54.

Agassiz and the Fish, by a Student

It was more than fifteen years ago that I entered the laboratory of Professor Agassiz, and told him I had enrolled my name in the scientific school as a student of natural history. He asked me a few questions about my object in coming, my antecedents generally, the mode in which I afterwards proposed to use the knowledge I might acquire, and finally, whether I wished to study any special branch. To the latter I replied that while I wished to be well grounded in all departments of zoology, I purposed to devote myself specially to insects.

"When do you wish to begin?" he asked.

"Now," I replied.

This seemed to please him, and with an energetic "Very well," he reached from a shelf a huge jar of specimens in yellow alcohol.

"Take this fish," he said, "and look at it; we call it a Haemulon; by and by I will ask what you have seen."

With that he left me, but in a moment returned with explicit instructions as to the care of the object entrusted to me.

"No man is fit to be a naturalist," said he, "who does not know how to take care of specimens."

I was to keep the fish before me in a tin tray, and occasionally moisten the surface with alcohol from the jar, always taking care to replace the stopper tightly. Those were not the days of ground glass stoppers, and elegantly shaped exhibition jars; all the old students will recall the huge, neckless glass bottles with their leaky, wax-besmeared corks, half-eaten by insects and begrimed with cellar dust. Entomology was a cleaner science than ichthyology, but the example of the professor who had unhesitatingly plunged to the bottom of the jar to produce the fish was infectious; and though this alcohol had "a very ancient and fish-like smell," I really dared not show any aversion within these sacred precincts, and treated the alcohol as though it were pure water. Still I was conscious of a passing feeling of disappointment, for gazing at a fish did not commend itself to an ardent entomologist. My friends at home, too, were annoyed, when they discovered that no amount of eau de cologne would drown the perfume which haunted me like a shadow.

In ten minutes I had seen all that could be seen in that fish, and started in search of the professor, who had, however, left the museum; and when I returned, after lingering over some of the odd animals stored in the upper apartment, my specimen was dry all over. I dashed the fluid over the fish as if to resuscitate it from a fainting-fit, and looked with anxiety for a return of a normal, sloppy appearance. This little excitement over, nothing was to be done but return to a steadfast gaze at my mute companion. Half an hour passed, an hour, another hour; the fish began to look loathsome. I turned it over and around; looked it in the face—ghastly; from behind, beneath, above, sideways, at a three-quarters view—just as ghastly. I was in despair; at an early hour, I concluded that lunch was necessary; so with infinite relief, the fish was carefully replaced in the jar, and for an hour I was free.

On my return, I learned that Professor Agassiz had been at the museum, but had gone and would not return for several hours. My fellow students were too busy to be disturbed by continued conversation. Slowly I drew forth that hideous fish, and with a feeling of desperation again looked at it. I might not use a magnifying glass; instruments of all kinds were interdicted. My two hands, my two eyes, and the fish; it seemed a most limited field. I pushed my fingers down its throat to see how sharp its teeth were. I began to count the scales in the different rows until I was convinced that that was nonsense. At last a happy thought struck me—I would draw the fish; and now with surprise I began to discover new features in the creature. Just then the professor returned.

"That is right," said he, "a pencil is one of the best eyes. I am glad to notice, too, that you keep your specimen wet and your bottle corked."

With these encouraging words he added—"Well, what is it like?"

He listened attentively to my brief rehearsal of the structure of parts whose names were still unknown to me; the fringed gill-arches and movable operculum; the pores of the head, fleshly lips, and lidless eyes; the lateral line, the spinous fin, and forked tail; the compressed and arched body. When I had finished, he waited as if expecting more, and then, with an air of disappointment: "You have not looked very carefully; why," he continued, more earnestly, "you haven't seen one of the most conspicuous features of the animal, which is as plainly before your eyes as the fish itself. Look again; look again!" And he left me to my misery.

I was piqued; I was mortified. Still more of that wretched fish? But now I set myself to the task with a will, and discovered one new thing after another, until I saw how just the professor's criticism had been. The afternoon passed quickly, and when, towards its close, the professor inquired,

"Do you see it yet?"

"No," I replied. "I am certain I do not, but I see how little I saw before."

"That is next best," said he earnestly, "but I won't hear you now; put away your fish and go home; perhaps you will be ready with a better answer in the morning. I will examine you before you look at the fish."

This was disconcerting; not only must I think of my fish all night, studying, without the object before me, what this unknown but most visible feature might be, but also, without reviewing my new discoveries, I must give an exact account of them the next day. I had a bad memory; so I walked home by Charles River in a distracted state, with my two perplexities.

The cordial greeting from the professor the next morning was reassuring; here was a man who seemed to be quite as anxious as I that I should see for myself what he saw.

"Do you perhaps mean," I asked, "that the fish has symmetrical sides with paired organs?"

His thoroughly pleased, "Of course, of course!" repaid the wakeful hours of the previous night. After he had discoursed most happily and enthusiastically—as he always did—upon the importance of this point, I ventured to ask what I should do next.

"Oh, look at your fish!" he said, and left me again to my own devices. In a little more than an hour he returned and heard my new catalogue.

"That is good, that is good!" he repeated, "but that is not all; go on." And so for three long days, he placed that fish before my eyes, forbidding me to look at anything else, or to use any artificial aid. "Look, look, look," was his repeated injunction.

This was the best entomological lesson I ever had—a lesson whose influence was extended to the details of every subsequent study; a legacy the professor has left to me, as he left it to many others, of inestimable value, which we could not buy, with which we cannot part.

A year afterwards, some of us were amusing ourselves with chalking outlandish beasts upon the blackboard. We drew prancing star-fishes; frogs in mortal combat; hydro-headed worms; stately craw-fishes, standing on their tails, bearing aloft umbrellas; and grotesque fishes, with gaping mouths and staring eyes. The professor came in shortly after, and was as much amused as any at our experiments. He looked at the fishes.

"Haemulons, every one of them," he said; "Mr. _____ drew them."

True; and to this day, if I attempt a fish, I can draw nothing but Haemulons.

The fourth day a second fish of the same group was placed beside the first, and I was bidden to point out the resemblances and differences between the two; another and another followed, until the entire family lay before me, and a whole legion of jars covered the table and surrounding shelves; the odor had become a pleasant perfume; and even now, the sight of an old six-inch worm-eaten cork brings fragrant memories!

The whole group of Haemulons was thus brought into review; and whether engaged upon the dissection of the internal organs, preparation and examination of the bony framework, or the description of the various parts, Agassiz's training in the method of observing facts in their orderly arrangement, was ever accompanied by the urgent exhortation not to be content with them.

"Facts are stupid things," he would say, "until brought into connection with some general law."

At the end of eight months, it was almost with reluctance that I left these friends and turned to insects; but what I gained by this experience has been of greater value than years of later investigation in my favorite groups.

The Serious Joy Scholarship

A Personal Ministry for Jesus Christ

A $10,000 SERIOUS JOY SCHOLARSHIP IS AWARDED TO ALL STUDENTS ANNUALLY TO ENABLE THEM TO LAUNCH INTO LIFE AND MINISTRY WITHOUT STUDENT LOAN DEBT.

THE BURDEN OF DEBT IS IMMENSE.

Graduates without debt are free to
answer immediately God's call on
their lives and are made affordable to churches and
ministries that need them.